Conversations with Wright Morris

NOVELS BY WRIGHT MORRIS IN BISON BOOK EDITIONS
Date of first publication at the left

1942 My Uncle Dudley (BB 589)
1945 The Man Who Was There (BB 598)
1948 The Home Place (BB 386)
1949 The World in the Attic (BB 528)
1951 Man and Boy (BB 575)
1952 The Works of Love (BB 558)
1953 The Deep Sleep (BB 586)
1954 The Huge Season (BB 590)
1956 The Field of Vision (BB 577)
1960 Ceremony in Lone Tree (BB 560)
1965 One Day (BB 619)
1967 In Orbit (BB 612)

In Preparation
1957 Love Among the Cannibals (BB 620)
1962 What a Way to Go (BB 636)

Also available from the University of Nebraska Press

Wright Morris: Structures and Artifacts
Photographs 1933–1954

Conversations
with
Wright Morris
Critical Views and Responses

Edited with an introduction by
Robert E. Knoll

UNIVERSITY OF NEBRASKA PRESS
LINCOLN AND LONDON

Portions of this book were originally presented as the 1975 Montgomery Lectures at the University of Nebraska–Lincoln. The Montgomery Lectureship on Contemporary Civilization was established in 1946 from the income of the James Henry Montgomery Memorial, an endowment provided in 1941 by the Ora Clair Montgomery Estate. The Lectureship brings to the University eminent authorities to discuss topics of current interest to the faculty, the students, and the public. The purpose of the lectures is to generate constructive thought on contemporary problems.

Publishers on the Plains

UNP

First Bison Book printing: 1977
Most recent printing indicated by the first digit below:
1   2   3   4   5   6   7   8   9   10

Library of Congress Cataloging in Publication Data
Main entry under title:
Conversations with Wright Morris.
   Includes bibliographical references and index.
   1. Morris, Wright, 1910–   —Addresses, essays,
lectures. 2. Morris, Wright, 1910–   —Bibliography.
I. Morris, Wright, 1910–   II. Knoll, Robert E.
PS3525.07475Z6   813'.5'2   76–25497
ISBN 0–8032–0904–5
ISBN 0–8032–5854–2 pbk.

Manufactured in the United States of America

Contents

Introduction

"The Art of Wright Morris" was the subject of the Montgomery Lectures at the University of Nebraska–Lincoln in the fall of 1975. While Wright Morris himself was on campus as novelist-in-residence and visiting professor of English, a number of critics and scholars were invited to the University to speak about his work and record conversations about his craft and artistic principles. They came successively from October until December, remaining for two- and three-day visits. Each lecture and conversation was a unit, the conversation growing from issues proposed in the lecture.

CONVERSATIONS WITH WRIGHT MORRIS contains three Montgomery Lectures, records of four conversations, a concluding essay by the novelist, and a bibliography. The addresses appear as they were delivered, without change in style. They have the immediacy of oral presentation, the relative informality of the lecture platform, and the tone of friend talking to friend. Similarly, the conversations are printed here essentially as they occurred; and though they have been edited for clarity, they retain their spontaneous vigor. Morris has himself helped with editing them. This continuing exchange between a distinguished practicing novelist at the peak of his career and his critics should be of unique value to students of American fiction, to devotees of Wright Morris, and to general readers. Here the artist and the student of art confront one another in friendly candor.

The Montgomery Lecturers on "The Art of Wright Morris" were John W. Aldridge, professor of English, University of Michigan, Ann Arbor; Wayne C. Booth, George M. Pullman professor of English, the University of Chicago; Peter C. Bunnell, David Hunter McAlpin professor of the history of photography and modern art and Director, The Art Museum, Princeton University; and David Madden, novelist and writer-in-residence, Louisiana State University, Baton Rouge. Granville Hicks, editor and critic, New York City, was forced to cancel his scheduled visit because of illness. Lee C. Lemon, professor of English at the University of Nebraska–Lincoln surveyed Morris's critical writing, and Robert L. Boyce of the University Libraries prepared a bibliography.

Since Wright Morris is an important photographer as well as an eminent novelist, the Sheldon Memorial Art Gallery from October 21 until November 16 presented a major retrospective show of more than two hundred of Morris's photographs and published a sumptuous catalogue which Jim Alinder designed. Alinder also made the prints for the exhibition. Subsequent to its appearance at the Sheldon Gallery, this show toured nationally.

In the fall of 1975 there were other Wright Morris events. The University of Nebraska Press, continuing its program of publishing the Morris novels in paperback, brought out *My Uncle Dudley* (1942). The Nebraska Educational Television Network in cooperation with the author made a two-part program, "Wright Morris / Repossession," which is being shown widely. During the fall Morris himself delivered a number of lectures in Lincoln and in the state. CONVERSATIONS WITH WRIGHT MORRIS commemorates these activities and celebrates the accomplishments of a long career.

II

It is appropriate that the University of Nebraska–Lincoln should have been host to a semester-long celebration of Wright Morris. Born in Nebraska, Morris spent the first, formative years of his life in various whistle-stops along the Platte Valley, in Omaha, and in Madison County; and while he is in no sense a regional novelist he has continued to draw on his experience of the West for his fiction and photographs. Three of his four volumes of photo-texts record the plains experience; and he himself has said, "The books I have written, and hope to write, are apt to bear, on close examination, the stamp of an object made on the plains." He goes on, "The characteristics of this region have conditioned what I see, what I look for, and what I find in the world to write about."

Using this experience and extending it, Morris has sustained a body of work hardly matched in modern American letters. Over a period of more than thirty-five years he has published more than two dozen volumes of fiction, criticism, and photographs. From the beginning he has had critical respect. But though he is recognized as one of the leading novelists of his generation, he has not had a matching popular success. One may legitimately ask why. Even in home territory his work has not been well known. It may be that Morris's fictional strengths are also his weaknesses and that his highest virtues appear as limitations.

The Morris novels—and the pictures too—are not in the fashionable mode. Morris is less interested in an event, a happening, than he is in its implications. Lots of exciting events occur in his stories—tornadoes strike, bombs threaten to explode, old men die, young men assert their manhood—but we are not asked to participate in them. We are invited to search them for meaning.

In a generation whose popular fiction strives to be as close to journalism as possible, whose yearning for aesthetic distance is near absolute zero, this deliberate withdrawal from participation is uncommon. Readers conditioned to reportorial novels may not know how to respond to Morris's lyricism. These novels are poems.

The modern American novel is urban and peopled with sophisticated city types. Morris writes characteristically of westerners, small communities, open areas. Frequently very funny indeed, his novels are closer to the frontier tall tale than to the wisecracking anecdote of the stand-up comedian. They are humorous rather than witty, and they are in the folk tradition of Mark Twain as much as in the literary tradition of Henry James. The Morris novel is usually a report of picaresque adventure. A group of persons—sometimes the group is made up of only two but often it is larger—start out for some far place and encounter a series of curious, even bizarre adventures. When they arrive at their destination, they find the place different from what they had anticipated, and they turn away in puzzlement, disappointment, or enlightenment. The stories suggest something of the epic sweep of the West; and like the talk of frontiersmen, the comedy and tragedy are both deadpan. Its subtlety can be missed by those whose ears are deafened by the screaming headlines of an insistent present.

To date Morris has published more than twenty volumes of fiction. The size of this accomplishment sets him apart from almost all other members of his writing generation and suggests that his work might be read as a totality, as Faulkner is read. Some have thought that it is as hard to read an isolated volume of Morris as it is to read a single volume of Faulkner: for both, individual works illuminate one another. Characters from one book wander into another book, and incidents in one novel illuminate incidents in others. When the novels are viewed in conjunction, even as they retain their integrity they are seen to be interrelated. The Morris world is not fragmented, discontinuous, or rootless. It is of a piece. It has an overarching unity of imaginative vision.

In addition to lyric intensity and epic unity, the Morris fiction has several classic qualities. Morris considers and reconsiders only a selected number of human relationships: an old man and a boy, a middle-aged man and his old friends, a husband and his remote wife. He reuses a single situation until he has extracted its full implications. He deliberately repeats himself, for some situations seem inexhaustible to him. Like Degas, who found the ballet dancer inexhaustible as an artistic subject, Morris repeatedly returns to the dream of the American West. With a classic deliberation he repeatedly juxtaposes the generations to contrast their basic assumptions. Like other classicists he does not search restlessly for new material, for novelty. Out of his old fields he brings new grain.

Morris is a classical writer in another sense. His novels are not judgmental. He presents his characters in their situations, but he does so without designs either on our emotions or on our convictions. The author stands dispassionately aside from his people, simply exhibiting them. We exist and they exist and together we share an imagined, created landscape. What does an action "mean"? What does a character "symbolize"? The novels are as enigmatic as a Manet group portrait—as carefully observed, as passionately detailed, as skillfully organized. In both Manet and Morris the subjects are lost in thought, living their private lives, isolated even as they stand close to one another. They all have their unrevealed secrets. Morris, like Manet, preaches no sermon. He respects his people and his readers alike, presenting not explaining.

Altogether these are not novels to be read with the

television going and the record player turned to full volume. These are novels for people who respond to the art of fiction. They are for readers capable of escaping the dictates both of fashion and of contemporary events.

III

CONVERSATIONS WITH WRIGHT MORRIS has a continuing, uniting theme: the artist as American. Aldridge notes that almost alone among practicing novelists, Morris, starting from the plains, has taken all America as his province. He writes "with a sense of the whole of America in his blood and bones" and possesses a "vision of the country as both a physical place and a metaphysical condition." In his fiction one finds a " 'love of nativity combined with baffled (and sometimes angry) disenchantment.' " Morris, he thinks, is profoundly American.

Madden observes that though Morris exploits the idiom of the American vernacular, he does not allow himself to be limited by it. By modifying it, he achieves a poetic economy. His is American writing in which every sentence and every detail seem to have an equal ring of authority. The result is what Madden calls a "novel of meditation." By combining a narrating first-person voice with a more objective authorial voice, Morris is able to escape anchoring his fiction to limited American experience. He both presents native experience and distances it through his highly developed individual style.

In his critical examination of Morris's achievement as a photographer, Peter C. Bunnell shows how Morris makes use of the American scene visually. Sharply aware that meaningful artifacts are subject to imminent disappearance, Morris attempts to salvage them so that the singular American life which they suggest may be preserved. Through the presentation of the American artifact in photographs (and by extension in the fiction), Morris aspires to absolute values. Resisting mutability, he hunts for permanence in the furiously changing American scene.

Wayne C. Booth sees Wright Morris as an American writer as surely as the others do, but he comes on the work from a different direction. Booth is concerned with the technique of fiction; technique itself may be an American preoccupation—a sophisticated form of the American obsession with how-to-do-it. Booth sees that the novels are less a statement of doctrine, conviction, or theme than they are the dramatization of a character's developing understanding. They report on growth. In his discussion with Morris, Booth found that the novels grow from a seed of perception, some provocative hint in some tiny event. Morris is not teleological; he does not write to illuminate a formulated thesis. Rather he works organically, allowing a situation or a character or a scene to suggest its own way. A novel is no less a journey of discovery for him than it is for his reader.

Though neither Booth nor Morris say so, this search for understanding, this hunt for meaning, may be an American characteristic, a quality observable in much American experience and fiction. Huck Finn strikes out for the territory ahead, Lambert Strether returns to Europe, Quentin Compson examines the southern past, all in quest of meaning. They have no dogma provided by church or state or authoritative intellectual establishment to which they can turn. Their fundamental continuing principle is that each man must fulfill himself, each in his own way. Though "organic creation" can be discovered in other cultures, the idea of growth has a particular importance to America. Morris writes like an American; he searches and he does not expound. His characters act like Americans: they set out in their old cars to find new territory or revisit the old, and discover at last that they have followed the wrong trails. They return to their points of origin and start again. Change not stability, growth not construction, experience not ratiocination, intuition not logic, the fulfilling future not the golden past: this is American and this is also Wright Morris.

The art of Wright Morris is then the art of an American novelist. He is at home in his vast country, experiencing, and asking us to experience, this nation as a metaphysical condition. CONVERSATIONS WITH WRIGHT MORRIS is conversation about America, and about ourselves.

ROBERT E. KNOLL

Conversations with Wright Morris

Wright Morris Country

JOHN W. ALDRIDGE

Wright Morris may well be the last of our novelists to write with a sense of the whole of America in his blood and bones, to possess a vision of the country as both a physical place and a metaphysical condition. The literary tradition from which he seems most directly to descend—and it is a tradition shared with some incongruity by James, Twain, Edith Wharton, and Sherwood Anderson—may have passed on to him the materials of this vision, and it may be said to have been reconstituted in his work with very little likelihood that it will survive beyond his work. His immediate predecessors did not, on the whole, display much evidence of possessing it, perhaps because they belonged to a generation which, with the sole exception of Faulkner, did not so much learn from history as write from the perilous assumption that history did not exist until they came along to invent it. For what is involved here is a historical imagination, which is not at all the same as a historical understanding or even a historical perspective. The historical imagination functions within a double matrix of fact and illusion, actual happenings and fictive constructs built upon actual happenings, and it does so because it perceives that what the minds of a people make of a national or cultural past, what their powers of mythic transvaluation remake out of the past for the new uses of the present, may have the profoundest influence on the formation of their collective character. It was the mythic idea of its history that shaped the epic in Homer's Greece. It is the idea of its history as epic that has shaped the myth of America, just as it has greatly affected the actuality of America.

Of Morris's immediate predecessors there may be some truth in saying that Hemingway did not possess the historical imagination at all. It was the contemporary moment in its radical divorcement from history that almost pathologically absorbed him, and his personal myth—however closely it may have resembled certain mythic formulations belonging to our national past— was created out of the urgencies of his need to fashion modes of honorable survival against the threat of contemporary fatalities. It was partly because the precedents of the past were of so little use to him that his work had all the tensions of emergency improvisation. Its codes and rituals were contingency measures taken to help insure coherence amid conditions that were fearsome just because they could not be measured by precedent.

Fitzgerald had moments when the past gave his vision of the present a darkly elegiac dimension. But such moments were rare, and so often—as in the pontifically beautiful closing passages of *The Great Gatsby*—they had about them the flavor of contrivance, of something not quite earned by the imagination but opted for by sentimentality. The great expectations of those first Dutch voyagers to the New World—expectations, after all, that were finally so mercenary—do not really join with the holy illusions of the priestlike Gatsby. For a transitory enchanted moment they are simply thrown together within the clutching embraces of Fitzgerald's euphoria. And after we have breathed our sighs in

rhythm with his majestic prose, we have paid our respects for good and all to the poetic limitations of a
rather affected nostalgia.

Several of Morris's contemporaries have written brilliantly about various single aspects of the American
experience—as witnessed in the city, the minority ghetto, the suburban East, the rural South—in most cases,
materials recalled from a period of our cultural history
seemingly almost as remote from us in time as old
Scanlon's Middle West and equally as open to attribu-
tions of a half actual, half fictitious vitality and romance.
It is of interest that many of our novelists younger than
Morris have had little directly to say about the life of this
country and have sought refuge from conditions perhaps
too amorphous, too vapid, or too unbelievable to be
engaged imaginatively, through the making of fables
and fictions of fictions, their novels becoming more and
more narcissistic and self-consuming as the traditional
social nourishments of the novel have been depleted.

Morris alone among these writers has had the distinction of preserving a creative connection with a larger and
essential America. Yet even for him it is evident that the
supply of nourishments has diminished; the social fabric
has thinned; and his fiction has had to compensate by
mining steadily deeper into its own technical resources.
But then one knows, has always known in reading him,
that it is just this thinness that is central to his point. He
has been from the beginning an extremely conscious
recorder of the subtlest symptoms of our entropy, the
dying out of some epic and transfiguring vision of ourselves amid conditions leading to such a massive im-
poverishment of our sense of possibility that we have
responded with outrage or sought the revenge of our
frustration in atrocity, suicide, and murder.

The America one encounters in Morris's most important novels may or may not still exist. There are those

who will say that, yes, it is very much alive and well and living in Omaha. They could easily be right, for hardy strains of past cultures have been known to survive long beyond their appointed time and to take their place with the biological oddities which live on—always in lessened mutated form—to remind us that giants and dragons once walked the earth, that stretching behind us is a larger past from which we derive and incessantly re-create the legends of our heroic origins and stalwart ancestries.

But one thing is certain. The America of Morris's novels no longer exists as a territory of our collective imagination, and that is because the myth that brought it to life in our imagination is dead. We may think that the myth survives in the popular culture of our day, but we will be wrong. It is not even there in lessened mutated form. What we see in popular culture are imitations and prevarications of the myth, media entombments of artifact, cartoon facsimiles which may have the vague contours of the original with one essential element missing: they bring nothing to life; they no longer fire and transform our aspirations. The true artifact is a sacred relic, a thing of magic consecrated by ceremony and sacrament. It embodies the myth as a talisman, embodies a moment of life or history when suddenly something eternal happened, when, perhaps only briefly, experience came alive with meaning because it touched and activated new circuits of possibility within us, when magic for a moment overpowered our natural limitations; and we knew, like Gordon Boyd, that we could walk on water and not drown.

This belief that experience might at any moment achieve epiphany and trigger in us the energies needed for transformation and new birth—this undoubtedly had its connections with the dynamism of the frontier and those mystical regions of the second chance spreading endlessly ahead in both space and mind. Americans have always been a practical visionary people, and, early on, the vision of the extremely practical frontier became a fixture of our imaginations, so that we ceased to be quite real to ourselves except under the stresses of risk and adventure—or in fantasy lighting out from the void of familiar boredoms and dead habits to make yet one more assault upon the existential mysteries. For utopia to us is not a perfect condition of life. Rather, it is a vital state of *coming to* life, of incessantly renegotiating the terms of our contract with Fortune.

It will be obvious why it is that we reverence the time of youth in this country, and why for so many adults life stopped with the end of youth. Experience was meaningful only so long as it lay in the future, had not yet been had, and so could be conceived in relation to the sacramental promises of the fantasy. Only the young were innocent enough and brave enough in their innocence to believe this, and it was such belief that made possible the conquest of the frontier. But for adults who had lived to recognize that the fantasy was incapable of being embodied in the hard facts of life on the plains, the problem was very different. If the frontier had to be won, it also had to be secured and maintained, and that, amid all the bleakness and hardship, was no mean assignment.

A reality had to be confronted and dealt with, and without the gloss of the fantasy, the reality represented brutally hard work. In fact, it demanded so much that whole vital areas of the psychic life—any emotion or impulse that might have threatened to subvert the business at hand—had to be repressed, and the need for repression became the basis for a religion of self-sacrifice, endurance, parsimony, and rectitude, a religion trumped up by pioneer expediency in the name of moral virtue. But since in the prairie world it was the men who conquered and the women who secured and maintained, a sexual split was created which became at last a permanent national schizophrenia. Now it would be the men who in guilty secret did the dreaming, who looked back with nostalgia to the time when they could dramatize their lives in accordance with the fantasy of vital becoming, while the women would be the guardians of what had been territorially won by the men as well as emotionally won at the expense of themselves and the men.

In *The Field of Vision* (1956) and *Ceremony in Lone Tree* (1960) the grotesque extremes of such sexual polarization define the conflict at the center of the novels. There are Boyd and McKee and old Scanlon, and over there on the other side of the great moral divide stands Mrs. McKee, alone and invincible. Boyd and McKee are sleepwalkers moving steadily backward into the past, to those magical moments when Boyd tried and failed to become a hero and McKee witnessed and failed in emulation. Old Scanlon is petrified in the past, has, in fact, seen nothing else for fifty years. A human artifact, old Scanlon, old outlaw, old gun, captured at last and brought back to justice both dead and alive. Mrs. McKee belongs with a large and ferocious company of women who patrol the precincts of the masculine fantasy in Morris's novels—those spiritually gray grandmothers, aunts, wives, and mothers, feet planted stoutly on the earth, arms folded tight across vast granite bosoms, barring the gates to Godhead, making very sure for the good of all that nothing is ever going to happen to anyone ever again. It is all eloquently and diabolically expressed in that well-known passage from *The Deep Sleep* (1953) when Paul Webb, the painter son-in-law, experiences his moment of truth, which is also the Judge's and Mrs. Porter's:

"The first Commandment of the House reads—Thou shalt not give a particle of gratification. Thou shalt drive from the

Temple the man who smokes, and he shall live in a tent
behind the two-car garage, and thou shalt drive from the
bed the man who lusts, and he shall lie in tourist camps with
interstate whores, and thou shalt drive from the bathroom
the man who farts, and he shall sit in a dark cubbyhole in
the basement, and thou shalt drive from the parlor the man
who feels, and he shall make himself an island in the midst
of the waters, for the man who feels undermines the Law of
the House!" [Pp. 278–79]

In the novels that follow *The Deep Sleep* two things
that may or may not be the same thing begin to happen
to Wright Morris. On the one hand, he moves more and
more in the direction of black humor, as if to fend off a
darkening threat to his sanity through the taking of
comic evasive action. On the other hand, he evidently
comes to see, in the writing of his more serious work,
that an insanity is indeed already abroad in the land, an
insanity very probably resulting from the frustration of
the old dream of existential becoming, the collapse into
dead scar tissues of myth of so many of the imaginative
forms by which Americans once dramatized themselves
and sought transcendence that there seems no alter-
native now, no other channel for the discharge of all that
anger and blasted fantasy life, except violence as cold
and brutal as the violence of the West would have been
without the redeeming and finally ameliorating power of
the myth. Violence has erupted in all sectors of our
national life, and as the honest and sensitive artist that
he is, Morris has seen no choice but to confront it. The
events of *One Day* (1965) occur against a background of
southern Civil Rights conflict and the assassination of
John F. Kennedy. Where McKee might try to emulate
Boyd and Boyd, Jesus Christ, the adolescent psychopath
in *In Orbit* (1967) emulates an actor, William Holden,
bombing the bridges of Toko-Ri. So far as one can tell,
the Indian in *A Life* (1973), by opening the vein in the old
man's wrist emulates nothing—he is simply a force of

nature turned murderous, as the incessantly copulating flower children in *Fire Sermon* (1971) are a force of nature turned meaningless. But we also remember from *Ceremony in Lone Tree* young Lee Roy Momeyer who drove his hot rod over two of his classmates because he "just got tired of bein' pushed around," Charlie Munger who murdered ten people because he "wanted to be somebody," and McKee's experience the day he bought his new station wagon and "drove it home like he had it loaded with eggs." At that point, "four or five of these hoodlums in a souped-up Ford swooped out of nowhere right up beside him, guffawed like hyenas, then leaned far out to scratch their matches on the paint of his hood. . . . The grinning faces of those hoodlums scared him worse than he dared to admit. McKee had recognized the nameless face of evil—he recognized it, that is, as stronger than the nameless face of good. . . . What troubled him was not what he saw, but the nameless appetite behind it, the lust for evil in the faces of the beardless boys" (p. 50). Finally, in the same novel there is Etoile's angry outburst when the radio announcer says that nobody knew why Charlie Munger murdered all those people.

> "You want to know why?" she yelled. "It's because nobody wants to know why.
>
> It's because nobody wants to know *any*-thing! Everybody hates everybody, but nobody knows why anybody gets shot. You want to know somethin'? I'd like to shoot a few dozen people myself!" [P. 117]

A contemporary writer who is not usually considered to have very much in common with Wright Morris once made a statement which reveals just how surprisingly much in common he does have. In an essay called "The Existential Hero" Norman Mailer (yes, Norman Mailer) said this about violence and the Western myth and the relation of both to the national psyche:

It was almost as if there were no peace unless one could fight well, kill well (if always with honor), love well and love many, be cool, be daring, be dashing, be wild, be wily, be resourceful, be a brave gun. And this myth, that each of us was born to be free, to wander, to have adventure and to grow on the waves of the violent, the perfumed, and the unexpected, had a force which could not be tamed no matter how the nation's regulators—politicians, medicos, policemen, professors, priests, rabbis, ministers, *idéologues*, psychoanalysts, builders, executives, and endless communicators—would brick-in the modern life with hygiene upon sanity, and middle-brow homily over platitude; the myth would not die. . . . It was as if the message in the labyrinth of the genes would insist that violence was locked with creativity, and adventure was the secret of love.[1]

It may be that violence was *once* locked with creativity in this country, and adventure was *once* the secret of love. But clearly neither is any longer true. And that, in fact, is our problem, just as it is one of the poignant motifs of our contemporary literature. Violence now is the symptom of the frustration of our creativity, and adventure has been lost along with any secret that may once have been associated with love. At the heart of it all, let us say, is challenge and mystery and the challenge *of* mystery, and we have witnessed the failure of that challenge in the dissolution of mystery.

For those of us who are old enough to remember the very different past, there is nostalgia—the romance and sedation of age in Wright Morris country. For those who are not old enough, there is an unfocused and potentially lethal frustration over the fact that they have no past to remember and nothing in the present that will be worth remembering when they do become old enough. The young, therefore, have tried by other means to recon-

1. Norman Mailer, *The Presidential Papers* (New York: G. P. Putnam's Sons, 1963), pp. 39–40.

stitute the challenge of mystery. They have sought their
frontiers, their possibly memorable instances of magic,
in violence, sex, drugs, and transcendental meditation.
And they have seen each of these sterilized of magic even
as they have known them, because in knowing them
they have merely joined in technology's conquest of all
mystery, all secrets, have added a little more statistical
data to the void we inhabit in which all things have
become known and almost nothing is deeply experienced
or felt.

There is much humor and a rare and genuine kindness
in the novels of Wright Morris, but the dark strain has
deepened in them. It is also to be found—in different
guises and because of somewhat different provocations—
in the works we consider most original and permanently
valuable in the modern American literary tradition. It
arises perhaps, as Philip Rahv once said, from a recognition of "the discrepancy between the high promise of the
American dream and what history has made of it. [From
Dreiser and Anderson to Fitzgerald and Faulkner] the
inner feeling of [the modern American] novel is one of
nostalgic love of nativity combined with baffled (and
sometimes angry) disenchantment."[2] That has been the
troubled preoccupation of some of our finest novelists,
and inevitably it is also Wright Morris's—although it
should be said that he cannot tolerate without some
amusement the faintest note of apocalypse.

Nevertheless, his somber awareness of what has happened to us in the past and is continuing to happen to us
today cannot be entirely concealed behind the subtle
locutions of his irony and wit. It is perhaps that he is
holding in escrow the ultimate pessimism he clearly

2. "Introduction: The Native Bias," in *Literature in America: An
Anthology of Literary Criticism* selected and introduced by Philip
Rahv (Cleveland and New York: Meridian Books, World Publishing
Company, 1957), p. 21.

sometimes feels. For he has, after all, lived much, has found much cause for love and wonder, and has too much practical sanity to make final pronouncements of either hope or disaster. Like Warner in *A Life*, he has been "a good hunter, a killer only when necessary, a man who knew his own mind, kept his own counsel, and had lived in the manner he believed he had chosen, not knowing that he had been one of those chosen not merely to grow old, but to grow ripe" (p. 152).

If there is comfort in that achievement, there is also a redeeming challenge and mystery in the far greater achievement of his art—and in the magic still to be engendered in his works to come.

The American Novelist
and the Contemporary Scene

A CONVERSATION BETWEEN
JOHN W. ALDRIDGE AND WRIGHT MORRIS

ALDRIDGE: In your critical book, *The Territory Ahead* [1958], you talk about the American writer's difficulty in turning his experience into usable literary material; and you imply that he simply has too much material. I'd suggest that this has been the problem for American writers right up to your generation, but that now we have many novelists—people like Barth, Pynchon, Hawkes, Vonnegut—who don't seem to be making much direct use of American experience. They are turning more and more to what has been called fabulation, the creation of fables, the creation of fictions of fictions, parodies of fiction, and so on.

I want to ask you: Do you think that this indicates that these writers can no longer cope with American experience? About ten years ago Philip Roth said that one of the difficulties with American life is that it is so grotesque, so outlandish, that it outdoes the writer's inventiveness. In effect it nullifies his power of imagination. Do you think this movement away from the direct or realistic reflection of experience indicates these writers are in that difficulty, or have we in some way used up certain essential experiences so that they have become so clichéd that you can't really get back to them?

MORRIS: It is almost twenty years since *The Territory Ahead* appeared. I was at that time concerned with an overuse of raw material, simple American experience or regional experience or the personality that seemed to be present in most of it. Faulkner was doing something with one part of America. Who else?

ALDRIDGE: I think of Thomas Wolfe and Willa Cather.

MORRIS: Something had to be substituted for the regional experience that had already been processed into fiction. When I was asking the question, America had been "literally" discovered. Though not seen clearly by me at the time, young writers in 1955 were taking different directions. The whole concept of what could be interesting had changed for them. As members both of the American and the world community, they had begun to feel more than simply American sentiment. That question of raw material had already been bypassed.

ALDRIDGE: Why do you think these novelists who are now about forty-five moved away from this realistic, impressionistic attempt to reflect and define the essence of American experience? Would you credit Roth's statement with any truth?

MORRIS: Well, it has truth for the satirist. A certain type of humorist is handicapped by the extravagance of the American scene. The satirist forces his experience into the grotesque in order to deal with it. If his work is anticipated by events, then he has nothing that is going to shock. He must anticipate the public, not follow along after it. It is idle to attempt to caricature American life if the caricature is already there. I am appreciative of the grotesque in the American, but I draw short of making it unsympathetic. For me behind this caricature is an element that is essentially appealing, no matter how abused or distorted it has become.

ALDRIDGE: Don't you think that Bellow and Roth, to name two of the better Jewish writers, have an advantage in being able to draw on either childhood ghetto experience or idiosyncratic urban characters? I think Bellow tends to populate his novels with grotesques, people who are incredibly manic, tormented, angry, and so on. They just don't seem real to me—I don't know people like that. Black writers also have a very colorful, vital, intense experience to draw on. They have an advantage which most Anglo-Saxon writers do not have.

Then there is this other group—and they would be highly offended to be put into a group!—who are working in black humor and the surreal; John Hawkes in particular. You, Wright, have a steadily larger element of black humor, a very gentle black humor. Maybe yours is only gray humor. You've always had a sense of the preposterous, of the comic possibility in the rather rough-hewn types that we encounter in your novels. But there is some point, maybe in *Ceremony in Lone Tree* [1960], where you begin to be more and more preoccupied with the outlandish; and in *Cause for Wonder* [1963] and *What a Way to Go* [1962], the whole landscape gets a little gothic. Some of your characters become almost as idiosyncratic as Bellow's. Do you feel conscious of this increasing grotesquerie?

MORRIS: What you identify as "grotesquerie" is largely a question of moment and circumstance. *Man and Boy* [1951] is the first overt instance of this type of characterization, but that's early. I wrote that in 1948. If I'd written the same thing ten years later there would have been more edge in that portrait of mother. That portrait undergoes the complexity of a full-scale reconsideration in *The Deep Sleep* [1953]. There I take what I felt was something of a caricature, a grotesque, and I say, Wait a minute! There's something lacking in this! That woman represents something that is absolutely inexhaustibly mystifying to me, something that is both individual and, in another sense, American. She represents a continuation of the notion of default in the male. Henry James talks about the default of the man in America and how the American woman picks up the pieces.

ALDRIDGE: I felt in rereading *The Deep Sleep* that there is more of the real malevolence here than I see in your later work. I think Mrs. Porter is not made hateful enough. You were too kind to her.

MORRIS: Your judgment there is at a great remove from the substance of my fiction. My fiction is not judgmental. I thought that in *Man and Boy* I had indulged myself at the expense of the human personality. It was too easy to make an absurdity out of Mrs. Ormsby—so Mrs. Porter in *The Deep Sleep* is a reconsideration of this woman. What her motivations are defy my analysis. She is not an assembly of human characteristics, and she is not merely a generic type. Mrs. Porter is unique.

ALDRIDGE: She resembles a distinct middlewestern type of a pioneer. Some of my relatives are like that woman.

MORRIS: This is not my conscious intention, but in being just to my responses, to my intuitions, I produce an authentic terror, one which you can not dismiss as ridiculous and absurd. She is fundamentally different from similar figures that the Jewish writers observe in urban life.

ALDRIDGE: They are caricatures.

MORRIS: Yes. Bellow used to be quite sensitive to the fact that characterization could become so facile that it would go over into the grotesque. But I sometimes feel that his talent as a writer, as an image maker, is at the expense of his characterization.

ALDRIDGE: He has much talent for characterization, or at least for creating characters; whether he really characterizes deeply doesn't matter. He's so fecund that he comes up with character after character who is strange and colorful and melodramatic.

Much of what Bellow writes about comes directly out of his own experience. In fact, it strikes me that much fiction now comes unabashedly from first-person experience. Almost always the persona-narrator is indistinguishable from the author—he becomes a sort of conduit down which wash the author's fears, and torments, and longings.

MORRIS: Once the conduit is opened up, the flow continues. This identification of writer and narrator seems to be where Bellow feels at home. He has seldom departed from it.

ALDRIDGE: The conduit really opened up in *Augie March*.

MORRIS: Yes. Where the writer and the narrator is the same persona, the writer waits for the experience to accumulate, then he processes it. For one reason or another this type of fiction is much appreciated today, and gratifies both the writer and the reader. It's a kind of confessional memoir that appeals on the level of the *roman à clef* to the intellectual, and the truth, the whole truth, and something more than the truth to the general reader. These readers do not want fictive distance. In fact, they want this "distance" eliminated. If they turn to my fiction it is this "distancing" that disturbs them. It is not the *other*, the fictive character they want, but the discovery or the confirmation of themselves.

ALDRIDGE: They want confession?

MORRIS: Well, they want the facts, the nitty-gritty. They want to dispense with the intermediary—but the intermediary is the heart of fiction. Through it the author reveals, rather than exposes, even about himself. On the evidence the modern reader-viewer prefers exposure, and that is what he gets. It may be a subtle way of reassuring us about our "immediate present." The distanced experience is something else.

ALDRIDGE: Does the first-person or pseudo-first-person writing these days exist because people feel that they can trust only their own experience; or if not that, somebody else's self-revelatory experience? Is this partly the result of the isolation people suffer now, their sense of solipsism? Generalizations aren't conceivable anymore.

MORRIS: The fact that we have a rash of this sort of thing indicates that there may be several areas of motivation. In a way I feel that the cause is not as complicated as you're inclined to make it. I think of the frailty of our ability to concentrate. We can bring very little intelligent energy to bear on an artistic experience now, and so we want the artistic experience to be immediate. We can easily justify our choices by saying we don't trust generalizations. We want somebody saying I, I, I—but a sophisticated reader knows that no one is less trustworthy than an I. In all of fiction absolutely nothing is so ambiguous and so ambivalent. In fact the only time the I-voice is really useful in fiction is when it is deliberately used ambivalently, as Camus uses it in *The Fall*, and there you ponder the whole novel to discover who the I is. Is it the author? We take delight in the perplexity.

ALDRIDGE: This is ironical, isn't it? In the heyday of the New Criticism people were saying that what we want in fiction is not *life* but *form*—that is, the ordered impression of life. And now we come all the way back to a demand for life as immediate and as raw as possible.

MORRIS: And yet this is just an exchange of illusions. No one is working so hard at illusion as Bellow. He knows, as any writer knows, that you provide one illusion of reality over another which, for the moment, seems to have lost its appeal; but both are fictions. I worked on this in *About Fiction* [1975]. We should be free of any idea that one decade is going to be closer to reality than the next.

The appeal of this immediacy is, I think, tied up with the competitive spirit. Let's take a character like Mailer —such personalities introduce our problem right away. Mailer, through his natural gifts and those sympathies which are modeled on characters like Hemingway, comes into literature with the established, built-in assumption that fiction is essentially an ego projection, a platform. So why in the hell should Mailer talk about *he* when what he is really talking about is *I*? And with his characteristic effort to be candid Mailer gets into problems because he is also a promoter. Basically he is interested in furthering the simplification of the *I*. He makes "advertisements for myself" into an accepted art form; and he asks, Why the hell trouble with the whole fictive pretense?

ALDRIDGE: He's not really a novelist. He's a fine writer, but I don't think he's a novelist.

MORRIS: He's a hell of a good writer. But what we're asking really is, Why should this mode prove to be so attractive? Mailer will be able to read Bellow, because he feels that he's getting less fiction through Bellow than he gets through other writers. Mailer does not read me because my writing is fiction, not well-or-ill disguised autobiography. I suspect that he no longer relates to "fiction." Somebody with a small talent but the ability to suggest "I'm giving it to you straight!" will persuade Mailer to sit down and read.

ALDRIDGE: When he writes about his contemporaries, he tends to favor people who are much like himself.

MORRIS: And a tide is running in that direction. There is no patience now for distancing in fiction: the illusion that we can dispense with complexities by simply saying *I* instead of *he* is our most abused conceit. The long history of literature suggests that only when we learn to say *he* do we learn to see *I*.

ALDRIDGE: Maybe most people are anxious for the authentic because they have so little in their own lives. They have so little sense of other people that to hear one man confessing something real—preferably agonizing—reassures them that experience is still out there and that it can be dealt with. We have a harder and harder time finding experience for ourselves, projecting ourselves imaginatively into somebody else's fictive experience. It is only when we feel that this story is not fictive, that this is right from the horse's mouth as you are fond of saying, that it can be acceptable to us.

MORRIS: This is an urbanized, sophisticated predicament. People in general do not participate in it. If I take a sampling of young people at random, if I dip hands that are tipped with honey into a group of people and come up with several dangling, if I did this in a non-urban environment these people would respond in a traditional manner. They would *not* put a story aside if they lacked instant recognition. They would *not* demand an instant serving. There's a parallel between hamburger chains and fiction—both strive to provide the instant servicing of need.

Now it was Bellow's particular gift to be able to meet this acute urban need. *Herzog* was read by writers and by readers who identified with Herzog. It was seldom read as fiction. The great pleasure it provided Bellow's generation was that of self-justification, self-recognition.

God knows how many *Herzogs* were being written, and how many were put back in the drawer. Bellow wrote their story. Who needed fiction? What one wanted was what one felt good after.

ALDRIDGE: Bellow's first two books were highly fictive in the Camus sense, not in the classic way; but he departed from all this and has never gone back to it.

MORRIS: Right. And why should he? *Herzog* was a mandate from the reading public, Bellow's public, that this was what they wanted, and it was what he could give them. It takes a great talent. If he tripped, the pack at his heels would trample him to death. In many respects Bellow seems to write the novels Mailer has in mind, but does not write. Bellow is surely one of his inhibitions. The urban drama of Jewish life is the only intellectual drama we have. But that may be changing. The "intellectual" content of even urban life is now too thin and faddish to be of dramatic substance.

ALDRIDGE: This is especially so when people are not sure what the real thing is any more. And it explains, to some extent, the popularity of the nonfiction novel which has been blown up into a major category these days. People want to be thrust into real events in an imaginative way. Normally they cannot comprehend the shape of events as they come through TV and the newspapers. When they get a sensitive person writing a nonfiction novel about, let's say, the march on the Pentagon, then they understand the event.

MORRIS: This is the most plausible audience-author relationship that exists. Capote touched on it in *In Cold Blood*. I am not like that. If I happen to write a novel about an assassination, everything that bears on the immediacy of the experience is irrelevant. I make that event instantly impenetrable, difficult to apprehend, impossible to find handles on: I muck it up into a novel; and it proves to be just as difficult to get at as fiction, even when it is presumably an immediate event.

I think this is a fashionable crisis, but the cinema has contributed its inestimable effect on what we take to be real. The cinema presents us with a look which both the sophisticated and the unsophisticated can accept as how things are. We feel when we look at a film that we're getting authenticity which does not require an intermediary. And so we come to the matter of psychic energy. Psychic energy is necessary to enable us to experience something that is *new*, or real; and energy that is used by the cinema can't be used for fiction. At one time anyone who was worked up, distraught, or bored had only the consolations of fiction. He might have had one or two other activities if he didn't read—possibly he could collect pictures or go to museums or study bugs or something of the sort, but the type of intelligence that was self-aware enough to want to *know* had limited options.

ALDRIDGE: All those standing in line waiting for the next installment of Dickens have been stolen away from the novel by the film.

MORRIS: They're gone, and they'll never come back, not in our time.

ALDRIDGE: You too probably saw a lot of films when you were growing up, didn't you? I did.

MORRIS: I didn't.

ALDRIDGE: In the thirties and forties we knew a movie was going to give only one very incomplete, largely fantasy vision of experience, so I did not find any conflict in going home from a film and picking up a novel. The novel was giving me the real thing, while the films fed my daydreams. That is no longer the case.

MORRIS: This is one more aspect of the complicated reality that diminished faculties have to deal with, or so we sometimes feel. Instead of developing more faculties to deal with more difficulties, we find our faculties are becoming more constrained—in some ways even exhausted—while the difficulties with which they must deal are multiplying. The other day I was talking in the faculty club about *The Works of Love* [1952]. We have a young poet here, a very good young poet, a very attractive personality. Like many young people, he speaks out directly and competently, but he was stumbling around over some of these questions. Suddenly he made the reasonably obvious but nevertheless important observation that among his neighbors he didn't know anybody as well as he did the people in *The Works of Love*. He said, Here I know all these people, but I really don't know them, whereas the only people I know are in art! Well, that's why we have fiction; and that, in the last analysis, will keep it alive.

Then the other thing: He had seen a Bergman movie. What was it, *Scenes from a Marriage*? I've not seen it, but it had made a great impression on this young man. Here was the question that any writer today asks when he sees a great film: Is the film threatening me? Even if you're not a film maker, you say, Hey this is blowing on my neck! So here it is. The film is not a substitute for the novel because the film experience is elusive and you cannot return to it instantly. But the writer must consider in his own way: here is a competitor.

ALDRIDGE: Don't you think the novel has benefited by appropriating filming techniques? You see them again and again in contemporary novels. Whether this is an imitation of one medium by another or some sort of simultaneous flowering of certain ideas, I don't know.

MORRIS: The film lived off the novel brazenly for half a

century, and now it's become adult, so possibly some of this debt can be repaid. Up until recently the film had little for the writer—except for a few like Faulkner who could appropriate film technique. Of course anyone can see how to incorporate certain forms of experience from a Chaplin film; but in the main, film had simply been a distraction. Now we can't help but be affected by a great film. If the writer sees a good film, he incorporates that experience as he would an actual experience and it becomes part of his psychic equipment. Sometimes technically he may say, Ah ha! and then modify his narrative methods. Consider the increased ease with which the dissolve takes place in most of the young writers. They don't trouble with transitions at all. You're just there, and there's no problem. An older writer might say, Here's a transition problem; but the young are already finished with it. They just drop it. I am not much of a filmgoer, and I am too critical, as a "writer," to see film as clearly as I should. I may have an instant sense of challenge, but I am slow to absorb what is useful to me as a writer.

ALDRIDGE: I think you've been absorbing film techniques for a long time, without direct imitation. You resort to a lot of filming devices.

MORRIS: You must remember that I'm a photographer, and in a certain sense I have anticipated film. I see in ways that are very filmlike without having been a film maker.

ALDRIDGE: I see a lot of montage effect in your fiction, and a kaleidoscopic rendering: glimpses, glimpses, glimpses everywhere, more than one thing going on at once.

MORRIS: Even reasonably obvious multilevel narration is actually filmlike. The film *does* what I have to simulate. The writer ponders how to achieve a film effect without getting into what is technically audacious but not really convincing. He can do what Robbe-Grillet does, you know. He writes as though he were translating a scenario.

ALDRIDGE: He makes a novel out of the filmlike experience.

MORRIS: Yes. He says, Let's see now, the car comes around the corner, and it comes and now it's a little closer; I'm beginning to pick up the sound; now it's gone; now look over here, oh yes, look at that shadow; it's just moving, oh, here it comes . . . here's the car now; it's a little, etc. He just gives us this, and he's intelligent and skillful, and the writer reads that with a sense of discovery, of more than novelty. It's fresh, it's there, but it was soon over.

ALDRIDGE: Yes, those experimental people have gone far on that one insight and I'm a little tired of it.

MORRIS: I think Robbe-Grillet's *Jealousy* gets through to the writer-reader on the imaginative level. He comes out of it, I think, on a slightly different level of consciousness than when he entered. An enlargement, largely on the technical level. The writer who turns from Robbe-Grillet to his own work will sense that he is making a nice accommodation of what he has experienced to what he is now doing. In short, he's learned something. Even though briefly. In this writer's other volumes his theories about fiction reduce his practice to clever exercises.

ALDRIDGE: We have talked about your kind of characterization in other contemporary writers, and we have touched on the relation of the film to the novel. We perhaps ought to deal with the relationship of the world around you to the subject matter of your fiction. I think, for example, that as your work goes on, beginning maybe with *The Huge Season* [1954], you have become much more aware of violence in contemporary life. That book is haunted by the bomb, and so is *Ceremony in Lone Tree*. Perhaps crescendoing in *In Orbit* [1967] you get a much more direct confrontation with the really ugly violence that we've all become so aware of in the last ten or fifteen years. There are instances in which you're dealing quite explicitly with that.

Is this new violence connected with the violence of the frontier to which you've recurred in your fiction? Are you suggesting that the new violence is the result of frustration people feel in not having a place to move on to, new challenges that the frontier once gave? The violence in those days somehow had almost a moral sanctity. We were bringing virtue to the aborigines, even if we killed them off in such numbers. Do you feel, when you're writing about these things, that there is a kind of metaphysic behind it? Are you saying that this is America without frontier?

MORRIS: Actually I am not that kind of writer. I'm not essentially a social commentator who looks around and perceives an emerging situation and then says, This requires my attention. What I have are preoccupations. The violence we sense emerging in my fiction is as unpremeditated in me as it is in the violent persons I write about. I deal with it thematically. I can't do anything but try to come to terms with it. I am part of the novel's predicament.

There are some interesting things here which I think will be true for me but not of many American writers, including the Jewish writers we were speaking of a moment ago. I am not an urban novelist. I am a son of the Middle Border; and however concealed, I represent a sensibility like Mark Twain's, right down the center. I will accept the absurd if I can see it in reasonably human terms, humanized essentially by humor. I will accept the absolute grotesque if I can see it in a context that makes it human. And in a sense that is what Twain did, but increasingly it has become an implausible way of handling American experience. When I began, it was still acceptable. We can see this in *My Uncle Dudley* [1942] and in some of my earlier fiction.

ALDRIDGE: But those are cheerier books, you know, than the later ones. You have a dark strain that's getting more and more to the surface.

MORRIS: Those early books grow out of my acceptance of the varying types of American "humors." These are not just midwest types. They run the whole gamut of American experience. The violence is essentially historical and it's not excessive, given the melodramatic situations. It's accepted as a fact.

God knows violence was not new—either to me or America—but the energy released in the postwar incidents, like the war itself, was on a new scale. I discussed it with my friends. One of them would have been Loren Eiseley. We often talked about this in both the loose and specific way of two men who don't have to explain their terms. And right smack at that time—we're both midwesterners—comes the Starkweather incident in Nebraska. We had read about these different cases, but we had accepted them as some type of social or let us say psychological maladjustment that really did not concern the culture as a whole. Two or three people had been under too much pressure, say, and so they crack up and shoot eight people in Brooklyn; or somebody shoots seven people in South Carolina; or somebody shoots six people in Alabama, and so forth.

But the Starkweather case occurred in a place and among people where it was almost pointless to use facile psychological explanations. It forced a reexamination of the clichés associated with violence. Most of our reflections were anguishing reflections. We were distressed in a way that the violence on the television and in newspapers did not touch us. What had been rather easily accepted became a problem. It was on my mind, and on the minds of my characters.

You remember *Uncle Dudley*? A nostalgically comic and picaresque situation—a car full of picturesque vagrants on the high road to adventure—suddenly shifts to the interior of a southern jail. I had been there just the year before. It had given me much cause for wonder. As the open road adventure wound itself down, I was aware that it needed to wind itself up as it closed. The jail scene would provide Uncle Dudley with a chance, I hoped, to redeem lost time. This is what we find him doing in the novel. For most Americans of my time "bad" experiences, like wars, occurred to be put into books. Evils could be exorcised by writing about them. Perhaps the writer will never be wholly free of that naiveté. I had been badly scared—as Huck Finn had been scared—but I knew in my bones I would survive it. Wasn't this America? Didn't everything happen for the best? To move from this state of ignorance to that state of disorder revealed by Charles Starkweather has been the mind-quaking move of my generation. Violence can be a life-enhancing release.

ALDRIDGE: But I think that the violence, if you can call it violence, in *My Uncle Dudley* is much cheerier. It's more remote. I don't think you feel the horror anything like the way you come to later.

MORRIS: Do you remember when the jackets of books described the author as anything *but* a writer? He was a dishwasher, a hobo, a "soldier of fortune," a migrant worker, a bus driver, anything but a writer. To *be* a writer, all of these real-life adventures had to happen to him. Jail was such an adventure, one of many often cited;

war was also such an adventure, if the writer survived it. Love, too, hopefully, was an adventure that might be experienced at home, as well as in exile. These and other ordeals that writers are born to survive were necessary to the prospective author. A little late, I left college and went to Europe. It more than measured up to my expectations, and I returned as a young man authorized to write—in my own mind. This ceremony of innocence passed away with Gatsby and Malcolm Lowry's Consul in Cuernavaca. Most writers now know that events do not occur with them in mind.

ALDRIDGE: Don't you find that you're getting to be more aware of the psychopathic nature of violence as the years go on? Take *In Orbit*. There you're dealing with a psychopathic adolescent.

MORRIS: I don't think of him as psychopathic.

ALDRIDGE: How do you see him?

MORRIS: I see him as a rather ordinary, ignorant, open-ended American juvenile. He has an opportunity to do what we think of as irrational. I consider him absolutely normal and his seeming psychopathic elements are introduced by the options within his situations. These options gradually prove him to be distressed and to possess an element of violence almost equal to the storm that appears in the book. The situation creates the violence. He is not violence-prone at all. He is merely another young man on a motorcycle, full of beans, and he's young, and he's ignorant, and outside of that he's Huck Finn. He's anybody that you're likely to find who suddenly one day walks through a door and says, I feel like something is going to happen today. I wonder what it's going to be. Maybe I'll get on my little old bike and go out and see what's going to happen. And then life begins to roll.

ALDRIDGE: And what happens is what happens.

MORRIS: To me, *In Orbit* gives a good—if small—measure of American life.

ALDRIDGE: I keep seeing more sinister elements in your work.

MORRIS: I think there's plenty sinister in *In Orbit*, but I don't start with it, you see. This is crucial.

ALDRIDGE: Is that a commentary on the whole generation? I saw this boy much more like a figure from *A Clockwork Orange*, completely mechanical.

MORRIS: Yes, the book excites that image in the first two or three pages, so it's almost unavoidable. But then I take the trouble to say, Look, that is how he *appears* but this is how he really *is*. He's just an ignorant kid, but let's see what happens.

ALDRIDGE: You take artifacts from life which are clichés or have become encrusted with cliché, and you freshen and individualize them. You take this boy out of the newspaper headlines and you make him into *that* boy. This revivification of stereotypes is prominent in *Love Among the Cannibals* [1957]. You consciously used clichéd material there.

MORRIS: Yes, that was very deliberate and becomes acceptable because it had the enthusiasm of romp, and I enjoy that. That book should have a great sense of energy in it. It's a book that should carry you along. You should not feel that the writer is skillfully setting up pins to be knocked over.

ALDRIDGE: There is a darkening strain as well as much playfulness in that book. The same rollicking occurs in *Cause for Wonder*, and in *What a Way to Go*, but I wasn't aware of it in your earlier things. You were never morbid, malevolent, but you were awfully serious.

MORRIS: I like to *think* the early books were laced with humor. They reflected my temperament, at the time sanguine, and my pleasure in experience—*any* experience. America seemed disorderly to me, but beckoning and rich. It had its brutal, its depressed, its disgusting side, but on the other hand it beamed with promise. It's the "but on the other hand" that dominates the early fiction. The first humorous touch of doubt is in *Man and Boy* [1951] where I am dealing with the mystique of the well-emerged Mother image. Then come the complications. Have you read *War Games*? That book was written in 1951, but not published until recently [1972]. I think it's full of surprises, even for the author. More than any other book it supports your feelings about the "darkening strain" in my later fiction. This strain is so obvious, and yet so novel, I was advised not to publish it at the time it was written. It features both black and charcoal gray humor.

ALDRIDGE: And that was certainly not in vogue in those days.

MORRIS: I can't tell you how unvoguish it was. That is hard to understand now. But out of that state of mind, we get these extremes of response that emerge with Boyd and Paula Kahler in *The Field of Vision* [1956]. Uncle Dudley's effort to become another person is a prelude to Paula Kahler's effort to become a completely different person, even to changing her sex. Now these are, in their way, extraordinary responses to American life.

This state of mind that makes itself felt a little bit in Twain was more felt in Melville, and in other American writers. There is a feeling that there is a force in American life; for all of its extraordinary buoyancy, for all of its sun, there is this yearning for darkness, for blackness. And even for a person of my temperament, which is as I say essentially sunny, this *other* makes itself felt with great persistence. Conceivably I would be the blackest black humorist—if I were not a son of the Middle Border. This is what spares me the essentially intellectual, essentially sophisticated, response. I start from scratch and build my mud figures and live in my mud huts, and then the storms come.

My concern is not to have these things in my novels brought to a conclusion, but to indicate that they represent states of American sensibility, of the American soul; and just as I am brooding over the alternatives, I want the reader to brood, too. I do not want to present anybody with a settled conclusion. The novels simply exist, like people you know outside the novels, like the writer himself.

ALDRIDGE: And that's enough. That's quite enough.

Form in *The Works of Love*

WAYNE C. BOOTH

I

Wright Morris has often told us that an abundance of raw material is not enough, that only in a technique that achieves imaginative reconstruction can fiction find a continuing life worth bothering about. Journalism and journalistic fiction will, of course, survive because of an endless supply of data. But fiction of the kind Morris cares about is made only when the facts are transmuted into something "out of this world," only when the floods of raw and spectacular events that threaten to overwhelm us are turned, through ceremonies performed in the artist's field of vision, into something more real than life itself. "Fiction is," he says, "the way it [life] is processed into reality." The artist is a man who is "there," but "there" is not a place reported on in the pages of *Time* magazine; it is a place where the territory ahead can only be found by those willing to risk the adventures of imagination.

To play with Morris's titles and themes in this way is useful in reminding us of how much that passes for fictional art is little more than raw report. But for many critical purposes the distinction between technique and raw material on which such talk depends is far too simple. Like many other paired terms that critics an-

cient and modern have used to cover the critical landscape—res/verba, form/content, signifier/signified—they
simply get in our way when we seek, as I do today, to
discover how an author imposes a variety of unique
orders on many different kinds of material, some of
them already ordered into art.

It is not only that all such terms are radically ambiguous, so that in every major artist there will be many
kinds of "form," even within a single work. It is also that
the full art of any particular novel inevitably escapes
any critic who pursues a general picture of a novelist's
"art" and "material," hoping to find *the* figure in *the*
carpet. Many modern novelists—James, Faulkner, Morris himself—have enjoyed playing with grand views of
their lifework, and they have thus invited critics to
ignore the unique art of the single work in order to find
and defend the kind of generalization we see quoted on
the jackets of Morris's novels: his works "embody his
attempt to capture and come to terms with the past";
they "achieve a kind of objective conceptualization"; they
"convey the quality of the American gothic"; or they
show Morris's "absolutely individual way of seeing and
feeling," "his humor and wisdom," "his sharp eye," and
his "clairvoyant vision."

There is nothing inherently wrong with such talk,
except when it becomes so habitual that we forget what
it leaves out. Morris's comment on his own works is in
fact generally of this kind, as when he says of *The Works
of Love* (1952) that it is "the linchpin in my novels
concerned with the plains. . . .the crux of an experience I
frequently return to but never exhaust."[1] You can't talk
of a novel as a linchpin or a crux without suggesting that
the structure of many novels together is more important

1. Statement by Wright Morris (November 1971), quoted on the
back cover of the Bison Book edition of *The Works of Love*.

than the structure of any one of them alone. When an author tells us in this way that there is a figure in his carpet, it can hardly be wrong to attempt to sum him all up, as I once did, as a Platonic dualist seeking to transcend the unreal raw world by imagining a reality "out of this world." I can remember feeling some pride in having discovered a pattern that not only contained all that he had written but everything he might possibly write as well. And of course I cannot and do not now repudiate my "discovery": how could anything anyone ever wrote fail to be covered by such a commodious umbrella? It is indeed only with an effort of will that one can remember how little any such general scheme says about the construction of each individual work.

Even when we have decided to pursue the form of a single work, *The Works of Love*, habits of generality tend to pursue us. Those of you who teach fiction know that if you assigned students the task of writing on *The Works of Love*, most of them would easily find a pattern of theme or image or symbol, pursuing "forms" that are in a sense static or atemporal or, as fashionable folk say these days, synchronic. The patterns are there, are they not?— patterns of isolation, of loneliness; repeated images of empty railroad stations, abandoned houses, forlorn railroad clerks; symbols of fertility (those five thousand laying hens, and the lonely man in the park feeding the pigeons with bread moistened with his own spit) or sterility?

Such "forms" *are* there, in some sense, for beginners as for mature critics. But meanwhile form in one special sense continues to escape us: the created sequences, the progressions from here to there, the unique patterns of experience and realization that are built into this work as its way of moving, ready to move any reader who can bring himself to move with them.

In short, no matter how many times we reread or

pause to contemplate the parts and their interrelations, we finally experience Wright Morris's novels as individual stories. In *The Works of Love*, unlike most of the others, we even experience a strictly chronological story. Is Wright Morris a splendid storyteller? Nobody has said so, though Leon Howard has hinted at it. But surely how Morris gets us from here to there, how he builds that classic sequence that Aristotle labeled with deceptive simplicity "from beginning through middle to end," is at least as important a part of his achievement as anything he has given us in the way of "vision" or "wisdom." Indeed, I suspect that we critics have done him and his potentially broad public a disservice by proclaiming portentous and often quite banal themes we have found in his works and thus understating his power as a teller of tales.

I seek to celebrate, then, in this general celebration of a great American artist, the storyteller, the maker of "plots," the minstrel who sings his once upon a time to us with a peculiar intensity and economy and resonance.

II

But what kinds of stories does he tell? The question is harder than might at first appear. What kind of a story is this one, told in *My Uncle Dudley* (1942), Morris's first novel:

> There was once an old man, a man who had every important human gift but two: "good fortune" and the courage to engage himself actively against the evils of the world. He was imaginative, witty, generous, loving, inventive, energetic, and enterprising, yet he felt himself to be a failure, and he feared that he would die without ever having achieved what he would most value: an act of true valor. But circumstance conspired with his own true quality to offer him a last chance, while he was still strong enough

to accept it, to commit a genuinely audacious and coura-
geous act against evil. At the end, we see him fulfilled, even
as he goes to his physical doom.

That is one kind of summary, accurate as far as it goes,
of what happens in *My Uncle Dudley*. But anyone who
knows the novel will find the summary strangely askew.
Only a critic like me, trying to make a point about
sequential form in a seemingly episodic work, would
abstract from the zany wanderings of Dudley and his
nephew a story that sounds like something by Conrad—
Victory, perhaps. Yet that story of moral triumph is
there, somehow, somewhere, as container or thing contained.

It was not there, as we now discover (see pages 86–87),
when Morris first conceived the book. Like his other
works, *Dudley* began with characters in actions, destination unknown; grew, as he insists, "organically"; and
when the act of courage was discovered, Morris found
himself, as he now says, going back over the episodes and
putting in preparation for that act—in short, revising
the novel to bring it toward—though not all the way
toward—the tale of moral triumph I have abstracted.
But the fact is that once the revision had been made, no
one could properly describe the novel without somehow
getting the climatic moral structure into the description.

Let us now try for a summary less abstract:

There was once an aging con man, broke as usual, drifting
from adventure to adventure, dragging his teen-age nephew
back and forth across the U.S., playing the chances as they
come. He thinks of himself, with characteristic deprecating
humor, as a "horseless knight. I got all the armor but I can't
get on a horse. And all of that armor shows I really ain't a
brave man." He knows that to act brave for the sake of
proving your bravery is stupid, but he is troubled because
every time he's had a chance to be brave "it just poops
out—it just looks dumb instead of brave any more" (pp.

104–105). And he tries to teach his nephew that to destroy yourself with acts of gratuitous display of "guts" is plain foolishness. But then, confronting organized evil in the policemen of a small southern town, and discovering a model of courage in one stubborn, self-ignoring prisoner who had made a career of spitting in the eye of authority, he sees his chance, his "horse": in full self-knowledge, knowing that he is quite probably destroying himself, Dudley spits a gob of tobacco juice in the eye of the sadistic head cop, and as he is driven back to the prison that he could have escaped by simply remaining passive, he waves jauntily out of the police car to his nephew, playfully signaling "the turn." The end.

This summary still distorts: it implies far more narrative direction, far less episodic material, than the novel shows. But it is accurate in describing a very special kind of story—a short comic-epic-in-prose with a resounding climax. An act of unprecedented bravery in the life of an old man is one thing, and that act is here all right. But that act as the spitting of tobacco juice in the eye of a fat, mean cop is quite another. The jaunty audacious comic tone depends on, indeed is made out of, the ethical force of the act, and that depends on the stature Uncle Dudley has been given by the end. But that in turn comes not only from the specifically "moral" actions that may have been conceived very late in the game. Our picture of Dudley's stature, like the boy's, is built of innumerable episodes that in themselves seem at best amoral, disjointed, and even trivial. Though Morris apparently began with Dudley's wild improvisations in California, as he conjures out of nothing both a car and a carload of paying passengers for the drive east, implicit in Dudley's conjuring is the formula that only the final act, discovered by Morris much later, brings to a proper climax: something like "the comic apotheosis of an American folk hero"—the con man as transforming artist whose sense of style, essentially flawed throughout a long life, is finally perfected with a gob of tobacco juice.

Few of the seventeen novels that have followed *My Uncle Dudley* end with actions as spectacular as Uncle Dudley's bull's-eye; fewer still bring a main character to his death or, like Dudley, to a point not far from death. To construct a formula for Morris's sense of an ending would be even more misleading than to deal in the thematic carpet figures I have decided, at least for today, to mistrust. About all one can be sure of, in approaching a new novel by Morris, is that in it some piece of life that begins by seeming radically unclear or problematic will by the end be clarified, or resolved, or even—most notably in *The Works of Love* and *A Life* (1973)—fixed for all time.

—There was once a man who saw his wife as largely a negative, inhibiting or destructive force. But as he observes her way of coping with life, especially in a major public ceremony honoring their son, killed in the war, he must finally recognize that her force is not only greater and deeper than he had realized, but that it cannot be judged in his earlier simple terms: she is someone who will "surprise you." (*Man and Boy*, 1951)

—Once upon a time there was a middle-aged professor of classics who had unknowingly spent all his adult life in a strange captivity—under the spell of heroic figures encountered in his early youth. Forced to think over the events of that life by the reencounters with those friends during a single climactic day, he suddenly and finally achieves his freedom by coming to understand the myths he has lived by. (*The Huge Season,* 1954)

—Once upon a time there was a young boy who was embarrassed and puzzled by—but largely indifferent to— the old uncle he must live with. Forced to learn and grow fast as the two travel through adventures that end with the uncle leaving him on his own, the boy learns both the uncle's true quality and his own readiness to become an adult, a readiness tested in the fires of the old man's knowledge. (*Fire Sermon*, 1971)

Such general summaries, which could, of course, be made in several different forms for each novel, can at best hint at the full magnitude-of-event that for Morris justifies a novel. We might even make the mistake, as some reviewers have done, of seeing the actions as slight, more suitable to short stories than to novels. But close attention to any one of his novels shows, I would claim, that to take these characters (and the reader) from *this* beginning to *this* ending requires a lot of doing, and that Morris is a master in the art of inventing the right incidents in the right quantity for the journey in hand.[2]

III

The full testing of such a claim, for any reader, will come not in argument but in the experience of the book as it grows under his hand. There can be no doubt that for many readers Morris's rhetoric errs on the side of spareness. He has sheared off so much—to use his own metaphor—that after one reading many readers report that not enough has happened, or even that nothing has.

2. That nobody has said much about this aspect of Morris's art is scarcely surprising when one considers how little criticism there is dealing with this aspect of fictional "plotting." The best work I know about the size and shape of short stories is Austin Wright's *American Short Stories in the Twenties* (Chicago: University of Chicago Press, 1961). The best on the novella, as something other than simply a compromise length between short story and novel, is Mary Doyle Springer's *Forms of the Modern Novella* (Chicago: University of Chicago Press, 1976). The fullest treatment of the problem of magnitude in didactic fiction is David Richter's *Fable's End: Completeness and Closure in Rhetorical Fiction* (Chicago: University of Chicago Press, 1975). The last two are strongly influenced by the major work of Sheldon Sacks, *Fiction and the Shape of Belief* (Berkeley: University of California Press, 1964).

It may be for this reason that we who admire the novels
are fond of saying, "You can't read Morris, you can only
reread him." Or we even echo David Madden's claim that
you can't read any one of the novels without having read
them all. But though it is true that rereading offers more
rewards in Morris than in all but a handful of living
novelists, I should like today to test a different assumption: that all he asks of us, really, is that we attempt to
become what he has called "the ideal reader." In *About
Fiction* (1975) he talks at some length about this reader
—at some length, that is, for a man given to short,
telegraphic paragraphs on subjects that many critics
would write whole books about.

"The novel requires reading," he says, and at first we
might think that he is simply climbing on the band-
wagon of recent reader-centered critics: Norman Hol-
land, Stanley Fish, Wolfgang Iser, Jonathan Culler,
Roland Barthes, and many another. But he soon makes
clear that his ideal is entirely different from the free
inventor of plural meanings that many are urging us to
become—a kind of rival to the artist, completing his
unfinished work. If we are to use the text as a stimulus
for our own inventive play—the sort of *ludisme* that
Derrida urges upon us—we are to do so only after the
most rigorous kind of subjection to the author's own
game plan. "Either the reader takes time to read what is
written, or what is written will suffer from more than
neglect." And the chief enemy of both author and reader,
he says, is speed reading. "These new skills [of speed
reading], among other things, mark the end of the
traditional relationship between writing and reading,
between reader and writer. The writer must still learn to
write (it is assumed) but the reader need only learn to
read faster and faster. Apparatus to speed up slow
readers is now distributed by book clubs, on the safe
assumption that club books are piling up behind slow

readers. Quick searching scrutiny persuades most of such readers to skip club books."[3]

Well, suppose we take such talk at face value and do some slow reading of *The Works of Love*, one word at a time, allowing ourselves to be shaped by each word and phrase as it comes, weighing it carefully and lovingly, as Morris did when he wrote it, discovering at each step the author's full care and love both for his words and his characters. To do full justice here, we ought to read the whole book aloud, line by line, as my wife and I experienced it during the past two weeks. Only then would we possess together something like the formal richness that Morris has created, and we would all recognize how much of that richness is left out of any critical account. Many of you have, I assume, already read the novel, perhaps some of you more than once.[4] But let's pretend that none of us have, and begin our slow journey with Morris's cryptic words echoing, "There is either time enough for what needs to be said, or no time at all."

I begin, as one ought to begin, with the title page, and I read, "The Works of Love."

The Works of Love? The *Works* of Love?

Already a vast domain of possible expectations, hopes and fears, has been ruled out, and the innumerable routes remaining are reduced further as we turn the pages—slowly—and read the dedication: "For / Loren Corey Eiseley / & / to the memory of / Sherwood Anderson / pioneer in the works of love."

Even though we may know nothing about either of these names, we do know that this author cares about his title, since he has repeated it already. And it is now probable that he is not using it in any simple satirical

3. *About Fiction*, p. 102, pp. 100–101.

4. In the question period it turned out that almost everyone had read the book before. But several testified afterward that they had indeed read it too fast, and that hearing much of it read aloud was like discovering a new book.

sense: it is unlikely that an author would attack Anderson's pioneering in dedicating a novel to him, so it is now probable that to perform or attempt to perform works of love will be a very good thing. If there are to be ironies, they will not work simply against the lovers—an inference that seems at first confirmed as we turn another page and find—three epigraphs.

Now most of us skip epigraphs. But if Morris chose them with as much care as he chose his other words, we ought to dwell on them a little. There are works, after all—I think of *The Sun Also Rises*—in which the author's own opinions appear more directly in the epigraphs than anywhere else. In any case, we have time, all the time in the world, to discover whether this one novel is among those that justify our time. So we read slowly:

Grown old in Love from Seven till Seven times Seven
I oft have wished for Hell for Ease from Heaven.
—William Blake

We cannot bear connection. That is our malady.
—D. H. Lawrence

If the word *love* comes up between them I am lost.
—Stendhal

Well, now, wait just a darn minute. We're in some kind of trouble. We just had love established as a good thing, and now, in the quotation from Blake, it is something to escape from, or so it seems; and in the Stendhal, to talk about it leads to some kind of disaster. *Will* the word come up between them, and if so, *who* will be lost? The Lawrence bit seems to take us less equivocally back to our other beginnings: if to be unable to bear connections is a malady, can we expect to find characters here who *will connect* or who *cannot bear* connection? Putting the three together, thinking about "connections," the word *love*, and conventional notions of how love relates to heaven and hell, we now know that things will *not* be simple here. Words will be dwelt upon, and yet they will shift under our feet—we are now more or less ready to turn the third page.

So we turn it, remembering to do so slowly, *thinking* as we turn. . . . We are in no hurry here. If we never read another novel but manage to read this one right it may transform our lives. Take it easy. Where are you speeding *to*?

We turn—and we find something that those readers who skip epigraphs will surely skip, something we find in very few novels, and in only a fraction of Morris's own—a table of contents!

Well, we've got time, let's look at it.

"In the Wilderness / In the Clearing / In the Moonlight / In the Lobby / In the Cloudland / In the Wasteland." Has the story begun? "In the Wilderness, In the Clearing, In the Moonlight, in the Lobby, In the Cloudland, In the Wasteland." Peculiar list, there, no matter how you look at it. From the wilderness through the clearing to the wasteland is in itself not so strange:— even if we don't know Eliot's poem we can see a clear rising and falling progression there. But how do we make fit on that consecutive list terms as disparate as *moonlight, lobby,* and *cloudland*? No way to answer that now, except to savor our own wonder. But let's not forget that the works of love we're to witness, if that is what we *are* to witness, will presumably move through these strange terms, out of the wilderness, into the clearing, and then on to the wasteland.

We turn the page, slowly, and find only seven words in the next opening, the same words that we'll find in the running heads throughout the next fifty pages, "The Works of Love," at the top, and in block letters, in the middle, "In the Wilderness."

Again we turn the page, again slowly, thinking still of

all our associations with that notion of the wilderness, and of failures of connection in the wilderness. And then we read, out loud, slowly, trying our best to think and feel every word of this narrative poem:

> In the dry places, men begin to dream. Where the rivers run sand, there is something in man that begins to flow. West of the 98th Meridian—where it sometimes rains and it sometimes doesn't—towns, like weeds, spring up when it rains, dry up when it stops. But in a dry climate the husk of the plant remains. The stranger might find, as if preserved in amber, something of the green life that once was lived there, and the ghosts of men who have gone on to a better place. The withered towns are empty, but not uninhabited. Faces sometimes peer out from the broken windows, or whisper from the sagging balconies, as if this place—now that it is dead—had come to life. As if empty it is forever occupied. One of these towns, so the story would have it, was Indian Bow.
>
> According to the record, a man named Will Brady was born on a river without water, in a sod house, near the trading post of Indian Bow. In time he grew to be a man who neither smoked, drank, gambled, nor swore. A man who headed no cause, fought in no wars, and passed his life unaware of the great public issues—it might be asked: why trouble with such a man at all? What is there left to say of a man with so much of his life left out? Well, there are women, for one thing—men of such caliber leave a lot up to the women—but in the long run Will Jennings Brady is there by himself. That might be his story. The man who was more or less by himself.

Now where does that place us—where can we go from there? The word love has not even been mentioned, though a lonely man—a loveless one?—and his women are promised. The wilderness of the chapter title is not mentioned by name, but already its feeling runs through these dry words about dry rivers that somehow flow, husks that preserve green life, emptiness occupied. The negatives about "a man named Will Brady" pile up, with no answering positives. So that when the narrator asks why trouble about him and provides an answer that is no answer—"Well, there are women . . . but in the long run Will Jennings Brady is there by himself"—we are left with the explicit puzzle: Why bother?

But we already have the beginnings of an emotion-charged answer. Why trouble with a man with so much of his life left out? Why, obviously, because the actual reader, as distinct from the impatient and insensitive reader invented and then dismissed by the passage, has begun to feel the sad wonder of such a life, the melancholy beauty of what this author will help us see in it.

More crudely: no author will raise the explicit possibility of the total insignificance of his hero without implying a magical act of transformation. We need not remind ourselves that ours is a century in which most literary heroes have been made out of such unheroic literary materials to realize that a strong promise has now been made: here will be a richly significant life, a life created out of seemingly lifeless places and persons. Whatever the works of love may turn out to be, we know that some folks will be insensitive enough to ask "Why bother?" This book will not be for them, because it is so clearly designed for us—those who will choose to join an author who dares toy with clichés as bare as "men of such caliber" and "gone on to a better place"; those few, by implication a select few, who will not demand heroes who smoke, drink, gamble, swear, head causes, fight wars, and lead nations. But to turn Morris's negatives to positives in this way shows another thing we have by now learned: words and things will always mean more here than they seem to. Obviously there is something curious going on when a trivial detail like "not smoking" is given this much weight. Not-smoking, like the other negatives, will turn out to be both literal nonsmoking and *something else*, just as the life is to be both insignificant and significant.

In an early essay, Kenneth Burke defined form as "the creation of an appetite in the mind of the auditor, and the adequate satisfying of that appetite."[5] Such an aggressively rhetorical definition of literary form can in the wrong hands lead to commercial degradations, and it is probably useful to supplement it with the notion that the author is making promises not only to auditors but to himself. Certainly Morris tends to think of his openings less as promises to readers than as problems for the author to solve, as he moves forward in an organic unfolding of what these lives are to mean (see pages 75–92). Whether we see what has happened so far as teasers to us slow readers or as solemn formal assignments made by the author to himself, we can begin to see that if Morris can fulfill his obligations, he will have offered us a strange and wonderful form indeed.

Consider more closely the promises he has made.

First, he has promised an epic structure without an epic hero. The opening solemnly employs the conventions of the life history of the representative man, the man about whom there is a "record," a publicly repeated story: "So the story would have it," "According to the record." We thus expect incident after incident that will carry the *weight* of epic, without genuinely heroic adventure.

We have been promised, second, that the epic will be of the works of love, while paradoxically the worker, who is in the long run "there by himself," must be incapable of lasting works of love. We will expect, nay demand, more of that paradox, along with some sort of clarification that will make it a paradox we can live with: a resolution, in

5. Kenneth Burke, "Psychology and Form," in *Counter-Statement* (1931; repr. Berkeley and Los Angeles: University of California Press, 1968), p. 31.

short, that will be both a great work of love and yet not a successful one.

It must not be successful, of course, because both the tone of the text and the telltale curve of that table of contents have promised—if not tragedy, and it surely is not tragedy in any traditional sense—at least some sort of doom or destruction, in *the wasteland*—a tracing of the "malady" of unconsummated "connections" into a "wasteland" which is wasted, we can predict, because works of love are difficult or impossible there.

Finally, out of what could be a much longer catalogue of promises, Morris has promised to produce beauty out of dryness: the two lovely melancholy paragraphs promise—if we allow them to work at all—a kind of prose poem in which the way a thing is said counts as much as what is said. We expect, or at least hope, that whatever happens will be offered in a style as rich—yet as spare— as this. Indeed, it is the fulfillment of the style in these few opening words that gives us our best evidence for hoping that the author will carry it off.

With so much that is predictable, why bother, as the narrator himself has just said, to read further? Well, all we need is enough confidence to lead us to one more paragraph:

> His father, Adam Brady, a lonely man, living in the sod house without a dog or a woman, spoke of the waste land around Indian Bow as God's country. It was empty. That was what he meant. If a man came in, he soon left on the next caboose. As a pastime, from the roof of his house, Adam Brady took potshots at the cupola, or at the rear platform, where the brakeman's lantern hung. He never hit anything. In his opinion, God's country should be like that.

What further riches have been promised here? They might be summarized in two words, comedy and surprise. Having expected a melancholy journey to doom (though a beautifully rendered one), we suddenly find ourselves with the dryness turned comic. The waste land we have not expected until the final chapter suddenly appears here in the wilderness, God's country, as a picture of a loner who may be pathetic, in one view, but who is also funny. And during the sparse episodes that follow, giving the life of this antiheroic father of our antihero, the mixture of pathos and comedy remains. This author, we are learning, offers his guarantee that surprises lie ahead among the works of love—as we see when we follow Adam Brady to his one and only court-ship.

He rides eighty miles east to find a photographer, has a picture taken showing him as a successful, well-dressed man standing in a rich virgin forest teeming with animal life. He broadcasts ten prints of this photo eastward, and on the back of each, "in a good hand, it was written that the man to be seen on the front, Adam Brady by name, was seeking a helpmate and a wife." When the tenth card produces a response from a forlorn "Indiana girl," Adam Brady replies to her inquiry in words that surprise us to laughter of a new kind:

> I can see very clearly your lovely eyes, with the hidden smile, but I am not sure that I, nor any man, might plumb their depths and tell you what they mean. I fix my own eyes upon you without shame, and I see your face avert for my very boldness, and I can only compare the warm blush at your throat with the morning sky.

"Another place," the narrator says, "he spoke of the illicit sweetness of the flesh":

> —I can say I know the passions of the men about me, and the heated anguish of the blood, but I have never tasted the illicit sweetness of the flesh.

And so, won by words like these, the Indiana girl comes west to a miserable dry life, appearing just long enough, you might say, to get our hero born—born "in this sod house, the cracked walls papered with calendar pictures of southern Indiana. . . . The grasshoppers ate the harness off a team of mares that year."

And within a page—again to our surprise—Will Brady is already full-grown. We should dwell for a moment on the two-paragraph history of the hero's childhood:

> In the town of Indian Bow there was a dog named Shep, who was brown and white and had a long tail, and a boy named Gerald, about the same dirty color, but no tail. There was also a depot, a cattle loader, several square frame houses with clapboard privies; and later there were stores with pressed tin ceilings along the tracks. In the barber shop were a gum machine and a living rubber plant. Over this shop was a girl named Stella, who ate the boogers out of her nose, and her little brother Roger, who was inclined to eat everything else. Over the long dry summer it added up to quite a bit. But in Willy Brady's opinion it was still not enough.

Not enough for what? Enough for some, but not for Will Brady? Not enough for a man who is going to be pretty much by himself? Why?

The second paragraph, considerably longer, is about what that childhood felt like, what it meant to Will, and it thus partially answers these questions:

> From the roof of the soddy he could see the white valley road, the dry bed of the river, and the westbound freights slowly pulling up the grade. These trains might be there, winding up the valley, for an hour or more. Sometimes a gig or a tassel-fringed buggy that had left Indian Bow in the morning would still be there—that is, the dust would be there—in the afternoon. Like everything else, it didn't seem to know just where to go. The empty world in the valley seemed to be the only world there was. A boy on the roof of the soddy, or seated on the small drafty hole in the privy, might get the notion now and then, that he was the last man in the world. That neither the freight trains, the buggy

tracks, nor the dust was going anywhere. But if at times this empty world seemed unreal, or if he felt he was the last real man in it, he didn't let this feeling keep him awake at night, or warp his character. He grew up. He went to work for Emil Barton, the stationmaster.

IV

Well, what is an author to *do* with a character like that? How can he avoid disappointing us, after all these promises about events which, in their "natural" state, as it were, are hardly the material for exciting story telling?

We have seen already how much his range of possibilities has been narrowed by the choices he has made and the consequent appetites he has created. Even so, there are still many different directions the story could move, and in its telling the author can choose from among many different shadings of success and failure for his hero, and of approval and disapproval, comedy and pathos for the reader. Brady could, for example, be led to one or more moments of complete fulfillment in love, somewhere in the "middle," and then on toward a tragic loss of that love in some kind of wilderness; or he could be shown to be as inaccessible to love as his father, never coming within miles of genuine "connection"; or he could be offered one or more chances at genuine love—some really splendid, powerful woman who, like May Bartram offering herself to Henry James's Marcher, could reveal his ineradicable weakness as a human being as he muffs the one grand chance; or he could find true love early and then, because of his forgivable deficiencies, gradually lose it, moving further and further into dark loneliness.

Whatever direction Morris chooses, he must also choose what degree of awareness to grant his hero. Is he to know what he wants, to recognize his successes and failures for what they are, and to see the meaning of the wilderness when it arrives? The author must also choose whether to create secondary characters who witness and understand the hero's plight. Finally, the author must make a choice that will govern all of these or be determined by them (in the finished novel one can never easily discover which): the various possible shadings of sympathy and blame or emotional indifference accorded the hero, together with the proportions of understanding or blame accorded his society as it makes or breaks him.

Here, then, is a curious openness of formal possibilities, at least as compared with what we find after the first half-dozen pages of most novels written before this century and of many even now. We cannot say, as we can after the first few words of *Tom Jones* or *Pride and Prejudice* or *Lucky Jim* or *Humboldt's Gift*, that the hero must not die. We are not even sure, as we are after a few pages of *The Mayor of Casterbridge* or *The Great Gatsby*, whether or not we are in the domain of the tragic. But what is not left open is the set of promises I have described.[6]

What Morris chose to do—and whether or not the choice was made consciously is no concern of ours today —was to take this great bulky nonhero, this unaware, unlicked, bumbling product of emptiness and crudity and turn him before our eyes into someone who, while still almost entirely inarticulate, has learned to see and suffer far more than we could ever have believed possible. Consider the unlikelihood that any boy introduced as Morris had introduced Will Brady should move in two

6. This impression of broadly open beginnings is confirmed by what Morris has said about various possible openings for various works. In conversation he recalled that in some versions of *The Works of Love* Will Brady lived on into further experiences in Chicago, and in one version of *Fire Sermon* he "felt fairly sure" he had "killed" the boy's uncle at the end. But now we find, that death as the conclusion of *A Life*, which, unlike most of the novels, seems to have been conceived from the beginning with death as its conclusion.

hundred pages to the ending that, with no possible qualms about spoiling an unspoilable story, I am now going to give away.

That boy has become an impoverished old man, living not in a sod house in the wilderness but in a shoddy rooming house in the waste land—which turns out to be, as one might have predicted, Chicago. But he has not become, as he might have in some other authors' novels, a helpless bum on skid row. He still has a kind of poignant dignity. He even has a job, sorting waybills in the freight yards. And he has his lean, dry memories. But what is most astonishing, especially if one considers it separate from the intervening incidents, is that he now exhibits a profound capacity to wonder about the human condition and to imagine himself into the meager lives that surround him. His own failures in attempted works of love have perfected his imagination: his own life is lived in the many impoverished lives that surround him. He has, in short, unlikely as it seems, learned how to perform prodigious works of love—but they are almost entirely works of imagination, never realized fully with the actual people he would like to help, and never expressible in his own words.

Here is how he studies their lives from his freight yard tower:

> In the windows along the canal the blinds were usually drawn, and behind the blinds, when the lights came on, he could see the people in the rooms moving around. Nearly all of them ate at the back of the house, then moved to the front. There they would talk, or sit and play cards, or wander about from room to room until it was time, as the saying goes, to go to bed. Then the front lights would go off, other lights come on. A woman would stand facing the mirror, and a man, scratching himself, would sit on the edge of a sagging bed, holding one shoe. Peering into it as if his foot was still there. Or letting it fall so that it was heard in the room below.

> In all of this there was nothing unusual—every night it happened everywhere—except that the people in these rooms were not alone. The old man in the tower, the waybills in his hand, was there with them. He had his meals with them in the back, wandered with all of them to the front, listened to the talk, and then saw by his watch what time it was. With them all he made his way through the house to bed. He sat there on the edge, looking at his feet or the hole in the rug.
>
> It seemed to Will Brady that he knew these people, that he had lived in these rooms behind the windows. . . . [Pp. 239–40]

One of the fine achievements of the novel is the way in which Morris manages to convey Brady's schooled imagination in words that Brady could never have mastered and yet that are as much his as Morris's. There's nothing new in this technique: it is simply one version of the *erlebte Rede*, or *style indirect libre*, or free indirect style that, as critics have recognized since early in this century, enables modern authors to convey a counterpoint of two or more voices at once. But no one, not even James Joyce in *Dubliners*, has ever used the technique with a more powerful combination of comedy and pathos than we find here. As in all *erlebte Rede* in which the protagonist is essentially sympathetic, the effect moves toward comedy when the character's voice moves furthest from the implied author, and toward pathos or poignancy when the distance is least. (There is, of course, a limit here: if they become indistinguishable, then all effects shift dramatically.)

Listen to my slow reading of Brady-Morris's account of one of the many visions that come to this unconsciously holy man, the man who knows little of his own true condition but a great deal about the lot of mankind:

> And then there were times—there were times toward morning when the city itself was as real as a picture, but the

people who had lived in the city all seemed to be gone. Every man, woman, and child had disappeared. The lights still burned, the curtains still moved in the draft at the bedroom windows, and here and there, like a young cock crowing, an alarm went off. But there was something or other missing from the damp night air. The smell of man—as Will Brady could tell you—was gone from it.

What had happened? It seemed that the inhabitants had up and fled during the night. As if a new Pied Piper, or some such wonder, had passed in the street. Hearing this sound, they had rolled out of bed, or raised on one elbow as if the siren, the voice of the city, had leaned in the window and spoken to them. Beckoned, whispered to them, that the time had come. Nor were they surprised, as every man knew that it would. So they had risen, soundlessly, and gone into the streets.

Still there on the floor were their socks and shoes, on the bedpost their ties, on the chair their pants, and on the dresser, still ticking, the watches they could do without. Time—that kind of time—they could now do without. They had marched off in the manner of sleepwalkers—and perhaps they were. They had moved in a procession, with the strong helping the weak, the old the younger, and what they saw—or thought they saw—out on the water, cast a spell over them. Perhaps it had been the bright lights on a steamer, or the white flash of a sail. But whatever it was, whether true or false, whether in their mind's eye or far out on the water, they had followed this Piper, followed him into the water, and disappeared. They had waded through the cool morning sand still littered with cigarettes, pop bottles, and rubbish, and without hesitation, like sea creatures, they disappeared. Nor was there any sound, none but the water lapping their feet.

So it was with those who had the faith; but there were others, even thousands of them, who wanted to leave, but they wanted to take the world along. They had brought along with them everything they would leave behind: magazines and newspapers, chewing gum and tobacco, radios and phonographs, small tins of aspirin, laxative chocolate, and rubber exercisers to strengthen the grip. Decks of playing cards, and devices to promote birth control. They had brought these things along, but the water would not put up with them. As they entered, it washed them back upon the sand. There it all lay, body and booty, like the wreckage of the world they had been departing, as if a great flood had washed it down to the sea ahead of them. In the pale morning light their bodies looked blue, as if they had been long dead, though living, and a child walked among them spreading sheets of newspaper over each face. As if that much, but no more, could be done for them. How live in this world? They simply hadn't figured it out. Nor how to leave it and go to live in another one. [Pp. 241–43]

This man, who seems to spend most of each day and night deceiving himself with hopes that we see are illusory, who cannot openly admit to his deep despair about all his wasted loves, who knows as well as the "big, friendly woman," Mrs. Plinski, that his son's one letter per year signifies indifference, but who encourages everybody around him to lie to him about how much his son must love him; this man who "always read the want ads, as a man who wasn't quite sure what it was he wanted might find it there. Perhaps somebody, some man or woman, was looking for him"—this man has slowly, painfully come, like Mrs. Plinski, to "know how it is." And "how it is" is, for him and his kind, a very forlorn thing indeed.

But it is also full of imaginative richness. The bleak emptiness of Brady's Chicago world, unlike the western Nebraska world of his father, teems with people. Though it is *almost* as empty of redeeming human warmth or power, what it does have, because of what Brady has learned, is a man who can imagine works of love. He can even imagine himself into a loving role that will provide for children what he has never been able to receive for himself: disinterested acts of love. He sees a want ad, "Man wanted for Santa Claus." He chuckles and even smiles openly (the only other time in the novel he even so much as smiles is when, his second marriage on the rocks and his young son drifting away, he looks into a clothing store mirror and observes a "strange smile" on the lips of the stranger who looks back at him, and the strange smile reflects his growing cynicism about married love— it is a sly smile that goes with cryptic remarks like, "I notice these new twin beds are pretty popular now"). But the chuckle is accompanied by wonder at the new possibilities for himself. Could he be the one man really suited to play Santa Claus? He has recently had another vision, a vision in which a voice from above tells him that "the great lovers" are unneeded in heaven. "Pity is the great lover, and the great lovers are all on earth." Now he will himself become a great lover. Having landed the job, he dwells in his vision, surrounded by wide-eyed children:

> The old man in the Santa Claus suit seemed to like his work. He would have paid Montgomery Ward & Co. in order to carry on with it. Out on the street an old man cannot hold hands with children, bounce them on his knee, or tell them lies that he will not be responsible for. Nor can he bend his head and let them whisper into his ear. Very much as if he, this old man, could do something for them. Very much as if he knew, like the children before him, that there was only one man in this world—one man still living—who was prepared to do certain things. To live in this world, so to speak, and yet somehow be out of it. To be himself without children, without friends or relations, without a woman of his own or a past or a future, and yet to be mortal, and immortal, at the same time. Only one man in the world could answer an ad worded like that. Only one man, that is, and get away with it. For in the world it is evil for an old man to act like that. There is a law against it—unless the old man is Santa Claus. But for this old man these things are all right, they are recognized to be the things that count; and the children, as they do in such cases, all believe in him. Some men will put up with a good deal, from certain quarters, for a job like that. [Pp. 264–65]

It is not too surprising that a man who can see all that, however dimly, is finally able to imagine a loving pity for all the damned, a pity that leads to a final "holy" embrace expressing his desire to be united with them. Standing on a fire escape landing over the city, almost blinded because he has overused a sunlamp to give his cheeks a fine, ruddy Santa-Claus Glow, he has his final vision of a hell which, in pity for its occupants, he chooses to embrace:

There was a bright glow over the street, and from these flames there arose, along with the din, a penetrating smell. The old man let his eyes close, as this was not something he needed to see. He could breathe it, like the carbon, he could taste it on his lips. It was like the grating sound of steel, a blend of the sour air and the track sound, of the gas from the traffic, and the sweetish smell of powdered Christmas balloons. All of the juices of the city were there on the fire, and brought to a boil. All the damp air of the chill rooms that were empty, the warm soiled air of the rooms that were lived in, blown to him, so it seemed, by the bellows of hell. An acrid stench, an odor so bad that it discolored paint, corroded metal, and shortened the life of every living thing that breathed it in. But the old man on the landing inhaled it deeply, like the breath of life. He leaned there on the railing, his eyes closed, but on his face the look of a man with a vision—a holy man, one might even say, as he was feeding the birds. But when the lantern dropped down, and the traffic flowed again, he did a strange thing. He went down the turning stairs toward the water, toward the great stench as if he would grasp it, make it his own, before it could blow away from him. Or as if he heard above the sound of the traffic, the trains in the yard, and the din of the city, the tune of that Piper—the same old Pied Piper—over the canal. The one that had drawn him, time and again, into the streets. So he went on down, groping a little, as he had no proper eyes for seeing, or for knowing that there was no landing over the canal. A rope swung there, the knotted end sweeping the water, heavy with ice.

There was no one on the stairs, nor any boat on the water, and only Manny Plinski, with a brown tweed coat, was there on the landing when they came to look for Santa Claus. In the pockets there were turtles and a postcard to his son that had not been mailed. [Pp. 268–69]

V

It is hardly surprising that as Wright Morris tried to tell the story of how Will Brady moved from the beginning I have described to that ending, he ran into artistic difficulties. He has made no secret of his having worked longer and harder on *The Works of Love* than on any other novel; indeed, he finally found that he had to trim a manuscript of about two hundred thousand words down to the present eighty thousand. That's some trimming. Without getting our hands on those lopped pages we cannot know what was cut—perhaps it was mostly extensions of what we have now. But for our purposes it is enough to see how large a problem would face any writer who tried to join those two ends into a satisfactory whole. How do you turn a boy like that into a man like that, through stages that will seem both to the artist and to the sympathetic reader a probable sequence emotionally powerful in detail? How do you transform a man "with most of his life left out" into someone capable of Brady's final illuminations? More particularly, if you keep him, as you must, ineffectual in every effort at a loving encounter, how do you build and maintain the reader's sympathy for him?

As many of you know, Morris is only one of hundreds, perhaps thousands, of modern novelists who have attempted plots with something like the form this beginning and ending suggest: from ignorance or innocence to knowledge or experience or wisdom, from naive misguided hopefulness to a disillusioned or even despairing vision of truth, from damnation to salvation: in general, from a mistaken or inferior condition of mind or soul to a superior one. Success in these quests for meaning can come with a wide variety of what might be called physical destinies: death or renewed life, material success or complete failure, acceptance by others or complete rejection; and the spiritual success which marks such forms may bring with it either happiness (as in several of Saul Bellow's latest novels) or despair, even suicidal despair when the vision achieved is of an intolerable human misery or of the Void; or it may bring some curious combination of happiness and despair, as in the complex ending we have just seen. These differences can of course bring with them great differences in our experience of the quest for meaning itself. But it is surprising how such a quest, whenever it is central to a work, will render us relatively indifferent about whether a character lives or dies, or whether he finally gets the pot of gold or lives in a garret. The achieved vision becomes a fate we care about, and other aspects of fate become for us as insignificant as they will always have become for the character who knows that everything else in his life pales before the significance of his vision.

What does matter to us, given a beginning as empty as Brady's and an ending as full, is the quality of the "middle," the sequence of events leading the character over such a vast distance. That sequence need not be made up of casual connections of the kind that marked classical plots. Since the true progression is in *what the hero knows* and not in what happens to him, chance can play a strong, even dominant role in determining what the world will offer for the hero's spirit to work on. But what is "necessary"—to use Aristotle's good old word for the best kind of connections—is that every response made by the protagonist be appropriate to his character at that point and to the nature of the challenge, and that the challenges be of such a kind, and in such a sequence, that *this* hero can plausibly be led by them in his progress toward illumination.

The theory of such plots is not our concern today, except to lead us as deep as possible into this one splendid construction. If there were time, I would enjoy describing many of the brilliant inventions Morris uses to connect Brady's beginnings to his ultimate fate: a sequence of women, from Will's rejection by two whores he proposes to, through two marriages, on to a string of god-awful harridans who answer his ad, "Father seeks matronly woman as companion to growing boy," and finally to the kindly, melancholy, coping souls who surround his life at the end; a sequence of children, from his own baffling adopted son through his even more baffling child-bride, and the dirty urchin who sells him kisses for pennies, on to the half-wit, Manny, whom Brady conceals beneath Santa Claus's throne, blowing up the balloons that Brady hands to all the children who finally, indiscriminately, love him; a sequence of would-be tycoons, "big thinkers," ranging from those who convince Brady that he is a man of high caliber to Brady himself, who finally has himself paged in a hotel lobby in order to hear his name called; a sequence of encounters with civilization in the "east"—that is, toward Chicago.

But any one of these sequences would require more than an hour in itself, if I tried to show that it is either essential or useful in Brady's saga, and also that it is handled in a manner superior to the sequences in many another novel of spiritual quest. Today we have time only for a glimpse or two at what Morris does with those he has "promised" most openly—Brady's women—and then a brief look at how he handles Brady's son.

Brady's closest approach to love with a woman occurs as he moves from the wilderness to the clearing, just after Mrs. Ethel Bassett, a widow, has maneuvered him into marriage. They go to Colorado Springs for their honeymoon, and when Will Brady prepares to undertake his conjugal duties and receive his conjugal reward, he has a strange experience.

They went to Colorado Springs, where he sat in the lobby, reading the latest Denver papers, and giving her time, as he said to himself, to compose herself. A little after ten o'clock he went up, and as he opened the door he saw her, seated at her dressing-table, her face in the mirror. The eyes were wide and blank, just as they were in the pie case [where he had first noticed them]. She did not smile, nor make any sign that she recognized him. Could he bring her something, he asked, but when she neither moved nor seemed to hear him, he closed the door and walked to the end of the hall. There was a balcony there, facing the mountains, and maybe he stood there for some time, for when he came back to the room, the lights were off. He did not turn them on, but quietly undressed in the dark.

As he had never been married before, or spent a night in bed with a married woman, there were many things, perhaps, that he didn't know much about. That was why he was able to lie there, all night, and think about it. The woman beside him, his wife, was rolled up tight in the sheet. She had used the sheet on top for this purpose so that he was lying next to the blanket, a woolly one, and perhaps that helped keep him awake. She seemed to be wrapped from head to foot, as mummies are wrapped. It occurred to him that something like that takes a good deal of practice, just as it took practice to lie, wrapped up like a mummy, all night. It took practice, and it also took something else. It took fear. This woman he had married was scared to death. [Pp. 52–53]

Now it doesn't take much imagination to imagine a rough western man who would be mainly upset or angry or disappointed at a moment like that. But it takes an imagination of a special kind indeed to imagine a Will Brady who can *almost* create out of such a moment a successful work of love. As the book says, reporting

Brady's thoughts and the author's voice at the same time:

> When a person is scared that bad, what can you do? You can lie awake, for one thing, in case this person might be lonely, or, like Opal Mason, in case she didn't like men who fell asleep. But it was hard to picture Opal Mason rolled up in a sheet. Or what it was now in this room that frightened this woman. As he had never been married before, he was not as upset as he might have been, for it occurred to him that there might be something he hadn't been told. In the marriage of widows, perhaps, a ceremony. A ritual that called for spending one night rolled up in a sheet. He had heard of such things. It was something he could think about. There was also the fact that this woman was a Bohemian, a foreigner, and perhaps she had foreign ways. But nobody had told him. And while he wondered, she fell asleep. [P. 53]

He then thinks of the life of her first husband, of their life together, night after night with her rolled into that sheet. "It didn't strike him as funny," though clearly the rest of us see humor mixed with the pathos. "If a woman has lived twelve years with a man, and the nights of those years rolled up in a sheet, and this woman was now your wife, it deserved serious thought. And while he thought, this woman, his wife, snored heavily."

He gets up and stands on the balcony, looking at Pike's Peak. Finally, toward morning he dresses in the bathroom, closes the door to the balcony to protect her face from the dawn.

> What did he feel? What he seemed to feel was concern for her. Neither anger nor dislike, nor the emotions of a man who had been a fool. No, he felt a certain wonder, what you might call pity, for this man once her husband, now dead, and for this woman, his wife, who was still scared to death. He felt it, that is, for both of them. They were out of the world, certainly—but in what world were they living? Greater than his anger, and his disappointment, was the wonder that he felt that there were such people, and that

they seemed to live, as he did, in the same world. Their days in the open, but their nights wrapped up in a sheet.

Practicaly speaking, a honeymoon is where you adjust yourself to something, and Will Brady managed this adjustment in two weeks. He worked at it. He gave it everything he had. He learned to sleep, or to lie awake, indifferent to her. And when he learned these things this woman, his wife, gave up her sheet. There it was, back where it belonged, between Will Brady and the woolly blanket, and let it be said for him that he recognized it for what it was. A compliment. Perhaps the highest he had ever been paid.

The truth was that he was flattered, and it was her own suggestion, plainly made, that he learn to do the things her red-haired boy had done. Draw up her corset, and fasten the hooks at the side of her gowns. In the lobby this woman walked at his side, her hip brushing his own, and coming down from carriages she seemed loose in his arms. Another compliment? Well, he could take that too. He had taken something out of this world, learned to live with it. He had discovered, in this strange way, something about loving, about pity, and a good deal about hooks and eyes and corset strings.

He had this concern for her, and she seemed to be proud of him. [Pp. 55–56]

And then for a moment we move slightly further from the language and consciousness of Will Brady, so that the narrator can make us wonder even more than Brady is able to:

If in three weeks' time two strangers can manage something like that, working together, who is to say what a year or two, or a summer, might bring? Who is to say what they might have made of something like that? But in three weeks' time he had to help her into her suit, with the hooks at both sides, and kneel on the floor and button her high traveling shoes. Then he held the ladder for her while she climbed into the upper berth. She was wearing a veil, the car was dark, and it might be said that the last he saw of the woman he knew was her high button shoes and the dusty hem of her petticoats. Whatever they had managed, between them, whatever they had made in the long three weeks, went up the ladder and never came down again. It remained, whatever it was, there in the berth. When she started down the next morning, calling for him to steady the ladder, the woman who spoke his name was a stranger again, his wife.

"Ethel," he said, taking her hand, "you're home again." [Pp. 56–57]

Perhaps by now I needn't labor over why this makes a perfect episode for *this* novel—not simply a corner in the figure of Wright Morris's carpet. Though there is wisdom in it, wisdom-talk simply overlooks the intensity of that story as *story*. We experience such moments as human reality, as events occurring to a man who is slowly becoming ours as he is Morris's. Dwelling in his failure, dwelling in his intense effort of imagination and compassion, we discover why the sadness of Brady's life is much richer and finer than the sadness provided by many other novels of frustration and failure in which the protagonists never come close to an honest try. This man really tries, he tries hopelessly, blindly, bleakly, but he tries, and he learns about love and pity as he continues to fail.

We see how he tries and why he must fail even more clearly as he reaches out toward children. The closest he comes to a connection with any child is his tender playing with the half-wit, Manny Plinski, almost at the end. But the poignance of his success with Manny is underlined by his repeated failures earlier in the book.

That there must be such failures as part of the education of Will Brady is obvious. But what kind should they be?

Imagine yourself, if you will, as the author of a good novel—the one I have described—but you want to turn it into a better one. To do so, you must decide many things, and as you turn to your decisions about children, you must, most obviously, decide whether to give this man Brady any children of *his own*. One possibility, for example, would be to give him a whole brood, like that other sad failure, the father in Christina Stead's *The Man Who Loved Children*. Or you might choose to give him none at all, making him a man who *longs* for a child. Shall it be many, none, or one?

I seem to hear a chorus from all of us would-be novelists saying of course only one, one who can be dramatized fully, one who will represent a single forlorn hope of a genuine connection.

Continuing with this game in which I hold all the cards, shall that one child be a boy or a girl? Which will offer the most likely chance of a connection and the greater poignance when Brady fails? I hear you answer as one voice: a boy. Third question: Shall that boy be Brady's own child or perhaps one that more or less falls into his lap and that he adopts? Fourth question: Shall we have Brady seek out an adoption agency, in his quest for love, or shall we have a baby sent to him impersonally by one of the women who has rejected him to run off with the father of the baby? Your answer is clear. Fifth question: Shall we show Brady trying hard to get through to a boy who remains mysteriously distant, self-absorbed, indifferent, or shall we show the child trying desperately to get through to a preoccupied and distant Brady? This may seem to be the only genuine question so far, since both directions would have their own kind of poignance. But the Brady we have seen will not accept lack of connection without an effort. And so we have required of ourselves a dimly-viewed adopted son, baffling to a father who, in a desperate effort to understand him will—well, what shall we have him do?[7]

7. This way of talking about choices is not, of course, Morris's way. And one can be fairly sure that though he made some choices

So far you and I have done pretty well in this matter, but perhaps we can restore ourselves to a little proper humility by asking whether any of us, once we had made these "necessary" choices, could ever have been able to imagine the details of the encounter as it actually occurs.

Having read a book called *Journey to the Moon*, Brady decides that if books would put a man in touch with the moon, perhaps they would put him in touch with a boy. A librarian he consults gives him—naturally—*Tom Sawyer* and *Penrod*, saying that they would give him a "good idea of what was on a boy's mind. That was just what he wanted to know, he said, and went off with the books." He reads them both in one day, sitting in his egg-candling room, and

> by supper time a great load had been lifted from his mind. If he could believe what he read—which he found hard, but not too hard if he puts his mind to it—boys were not at all complicated as he had been led to believe. When all was said and done, so to speak, they were just boys. Full of boyish devilment and good clean fun. If neither this Penrod nor Tom Sawyer reminded him very much of Willy Brady, that

"consciously," as we say, meaning with conscious calculation of effect, we can be equally sure that others "just came" to him, seeming right as they came. I feel pretty sure, for example, that Morris never even considered other possible professions for Brady than the one he has, which happens to be both a marvelous choice and the business that Morris's own father first succeeded and then failed in: raising chickens and becoming a "big egg man." I hope that our little game will have dramatized how little we learn about Morris's choices when we learn a biographical answer like that. It also happens, for example, that Morris's father had a real, not an adopted son, that he did not die playing Santa Claus for Montgomery Ward, and—we can feel pretty sure—did not stand all night in Colorado Springs thinking about his new wife wound up in a sheet like a mummy. In the end we don't care much whether Morris began with a real "egg man" and made every other detail fit a picture of Brady handling delicate white eggs with his huge, otherwise awkward hands, or began somewhere else and imagined his egg man as needed. What matters—as I seem to have read somewhere else before—is the perfected beauty of the whole.

might be explained in terms of how they lived. Penrod had brothers and sisters, many freckles and friends, and a very loving father and mother. Willy Brady didn't have all of these things. But if his father could believe what he read, all Willy Brady had on his mind was baseball, football, Honor, and something called track. In Ralph Henry Barbour's opinion, that of a man who really seemed to know, these were the things at the front and the back of a boy's mind. If he could believe what he read, and Will Brady did, it was coming from behind in the great mile race that made the difference between a boy and a man. But to lead all the way was to court disaster, as the book made clear. [Pp. 138–39]

But the guidebooks don't work with a boy who happened to be, "as Will Brady seemed to think, the complicated type," one who will look at him and say, "Why are you so different?"

Will Brady had been facing the mirror in the men's room of the Paxton Hotel. He had taken the boy down there before they went to the show.

"Kid—" he had said, then hearing what he had said he turned the water on, let it run. After a bit he turned it off and said: "Yes, son?"

"I don't mind kid," the boy said, "if you want to call me kid that's all right with me."

"That was a slip, son," he said. "That was just a slip."

"The name I really like is Spud," the boy said. "I always say call me Spud but nobody does it."

"What's wrong with Willy, son?" he said.

"I've been Willy for a long time," the boy said, and Will Brady bent over, turned the hot water back on. What in God's name did the boy mean by that? With a paper towel, Will Brady wiped the steaming mirror so that he could see the boy's sober face. His eyes, his mother's eyes, that is, were watching him. What did Will Brady feel? Not much of anything.

"All right, kid," he said, and that was just about that. [P. 147]

And so the failures mount, some of them amusing, all of them rich in pathos, all of them building our sympathy for the man who never stops trying, for the man who never stops "thinking" (and who never thinks or feels very clearly), the man who never stops longing for some kind of connection. It is often almost too sad to bear, but because of the sustained humor it never rivals in melancholy some modern classics that strive to be "the saddest ever"—*Under the Volcano*, say, or *The Good Soldier*. Thus though Brady remains to the end puzzled by the word love, though he never makes full connection with any other creature, he is—to borrow some enriched clichés from Morris's other works—a constant cause for wonder; he finally becomes a man who was really there, he achieves a field of vision that is as broad as all mankind, and he performs the ceremonies of genuine love, love among cannibals who never provide for him the huge season that might have taught him how to live in this world and yet somehow be out of it—without falling into total destruction.

VI

In some such reconstructions as I have attempted, adding as little as possible but at the same time losing as little as possible of what a full, slow reading would be for the alert reader, one comes to see how little we have said about Wright Morris's fictional art when we have described, however fully or accurately, his themes, his wisdom. It is not for the final validity of any one of his views that we read a novel like *The Works of Love*. Nor is it to discover one more example of the pattern in his carpet. If what the novels share were our primary interest, why bother to read a second one, or a third—or, for that matter, why should the author bother to write a third or fifth or tenth? But if what we read for is the experience of a story that is uniquely formed in each work, we can explain both our continuing appetite for more and the fact that almost all significant novelists have written many works. They themselves clearly have a hunger to encounter another kind of character with another story.

The Works of Love thus provides a peculiarly rich example of a relationship that we find in reading all good fiction: the reader travels with an author whom he comes to love and understand as that author applies his vision to the unique world of one or more characters. The resulting counterpoint of three views[8] is often more sharply delineated than it is here, where the loving but critical voice of Wright Morris can be heard only through the kinds of inference I have described—deliberately muffled by the *erlebte Rede*. Will Brady's thoughts and feelings are mostly beyond his powers of expression, and there is no other character in the book who can speak either for him or for the author. It is essential that this be so if the full pathos of his loneliness is to be realized.

Unlike Will Brady, we slow readers do not travel alone but in the company of an author who views this sad life with a humor unknown to the hero and a power of poetic expression that Brady can only grope toward. Morris's is a vision that sees, at the periphery of Brady's stumblings, certain people who might have schooled him better in the works of love, were *they* a bit better schooled in how to express their own powers: Mrs. Plinski and three other women I have not yet mentioned, who are there when they are needed—Mrs. Riddlemosher, Mrs. Ward,

8. If we distinguish, as in reading many works we must, between implied and actual authors and readers, and add the dramatized "readers" that some authors introduce (usually for mockery), the fugue may become very complicated indeed. See Peter J. Rabinowitz, "Truth in Fiction: A Reexamination of Audiences," *Critical Inquiry* (forthcoming).

and Anna Mason, the most important of the three.

Brady does not understand why the elderly Anna, a religious woman, attracts him so much. She is as mysterious to him as all the other women. But as a saint manqué he responds to the holy when it comes his way. The only fully peaceful moments of Brady's life, except during the brief period when he can work quietly and effectively with his eggs and chickens, are those spent in a small sectarian church, waiting, as he thinks of it, to drive Anna Mason home in his buggy.

> From where he sat at the back, beneath the limp flags, and with the stack of collection plates beside him, he thought he could pick out Anna Mason's voice. Anna Mason would have his mother's voice, and with it his mother's kind of religion, and a man with his voice, and his kind of religion, was not in her class. He didn't belong, if the truth were known, in the same church. But he was there now, he was sure, for a good Christian reason, and he had something like a religious feeling about the choir. They wore black gowns and sat under the golden organ pipes. They rose as one, the women at the front and the men, who were taller, lined up in back, and the sound of their robes was like the clearing of one great throat. They sang, and he closed his eyes and waited for the moment when they would stop and there would be nothing, nothing—till the first hymnbook closed. That moment always struck him as something like a prayer. He observed it, that is, as he did Memorial Day, and in that sense of the word he considered himself a religious man. [Pp. 120–21]

Another one of his visions, then, one in which "something like a prayer" goes out into—well, into nothing, nothing. But Morris, unlike Brady, does not wait in loneliness for the choir to stop singing. He knows how to provide more than those silences. His words about his holy man build a loving form where otherwise might have been, for many a reader, only an unredeemed world.

The Writing of Organic Fiction

A CONVERSATION BETWEEN
WAYNE C. BOOTH AND WRIGHT MORRIS

I

BOOTH: I've been wondering about the repeated patterns in *The Works of Love* that I traced yesterday. I'd be curious to know if you had them in mind before you wrote or if they came out of the pen as you were writing?

MORRIS: Let's first locate one or two of these motif-returns that you think of as patterns, so that we're sure we're talking about the same thing.

BOOTH: One main pattern that I argued for was the sequence in Brady's experience: a person born in emptiness, seeming to have no chance whatever of becoming a visionary, who yet became a person of deeply educated imagination. I can't believe that *that* wasn't part of your conscious planning. You began with a simple guy in an empty world who has very little chance of becoming *anything*, and you ended up with a man who, though he has not had a fulfilled life at all, has turned out to be fantastically imaginative in works of love—able to create them in his imagination though never able to realize them with actual people.

MORRIS: Would you believe that this was not part of my consciousness when I started the work on Brady?

BOOTH: I just want to make sure that we distinguish between what you thought about when you began writing, what you thought about by the time you finished, and what you have discovered since.

MORRIS: My style of writing is organic. I go from one page to the next page, and I read on the page how well or how poorly I am doing. I take my clues, in the main, from what I have done. I feel my way toward the book's form, as Brady felt his way through life. I do not formulate or plot out the story, then write it out. The seed of Brady was there in the first twenty pages, and so were his limitations. He grew out of what I was writing. I had to stay close to my "feelings" about him. The problems occur as he grows older, and the writer is faced with options. There were too many. This led Brady into the disorder that I had to pull him out of. He needed to stay in the context of the twenties: the Chicago known to him and the author. As Brady's life ran down I was faced with choices that exceeded my own experience, and I relied on the *tone* of his life, as I found it on the page, to guide my imagination. This is where fiction exceeds life. It makes, if possible, the meaningful choices. Brady redeems himself, and all of us, as Santa Claus.

BOOTH: You really did not, in those early stages of writing, foresee that Brady was going to learn all these things and have—one can only call them visions—these fantastic moments of insight? In the finished novel I find these visions occurring very early, as when, with Ethel Bassett, Brady has a vision of what it means to be afraid. A little later he has this moment when he sees his neighbor, Clyde Kirby, obviously a lonely, lost person, guzzling bread and milk alone in his own kitchen, and Brady imagines himself breathing in and out the same air that the other people in the world have breathed. I find in all this such a clear sequence of increasing power to imagine himself, with pity, into the suffering lives of other people that it's hard for me to believe that you didn't plan it all.

MORRIS: Let's think for a moment. I began to think about Brady in the mid-forties. In terms of what I had done, a sharp departure. A few years before, my father had died, in Chicago, and I was pondering his life, and how little I knew him. This led me to think about origins. In point of fact I knew very little. I had no "family" life. I had left the plains as a boy of nine. That I knew so little surely encouraged me to ponder a mythic past of my own, gratifying to my own needs and imaginings. I see now that the search for Agee Ward merely continued. Or rather it began in earnest. The sharp departure in tone is this *earnestness*. To keep it from being a solemn bore I have enough detachment to lace it with ironic humor. The first few pages were crucial. Brady as a person, not a concept, must emerge from the tone of the writing. Tone, for me, is like the key in music. When I have the key I have the flow and the assurance: I have tapped the vein. I had in mind the ultimate cliché of beginnings—a man born in a sod house, and the life that beckoned to him, if that was the word. Like my father, he goes to work for the railroad. I remember my sense of discovery in realizing that the flow of plains life had turned eastward, a reverse of frontier experience. I feel I have the tone of Brady's life, but little idea of the life he will be leading. Onto the pattern of my father's drift eastward, I superimpose the life of Will Brady. My involvement becomes obsessive. I lose all sight of the fiction in my absorbed re-creation. Such an experience either makes a writer, or breaks him. This went on for five years, but I broke off to write *Man and Boy* and do the photos and text of *The Home Place*. I have always liked to work.

BOOTH: I think one of the big differences between those of us who don't manage to achieve fiction when we try to write it and people like you lies somewhere in this organic conception of growth. My plantings don't grow, you might say, when I try to get them to.

But let me push you a little bit on what that means. It seems self-evident to me that you couldn't write a whole novel about the Brady who existed at the beginning of that book. That is, there simply isn't enough *in* him. You show that this is so in those first ten pages when you say, Why bother about such a man? There must have been—I want to go on nagging—not just in your unconscious mind but also in your conscious mind, a notion that a novel lies in such a man only because big things are going to happen to him.

MORRIS: With that phrase, Why bother about such a man? the first explicit note of irony comes into a tone that is otherwise very solemn. The consistency of the tone I seldom depart from is one of the problems of the novel. The ironic departures had to be very carefully muted so as not to question or ridicule the sober tenor of Brady's existence. When I say, What is there to say about a man with so much of his life left out? I mean the reader to understand there will be plenty, however strange. At the same time, it is a challenge to me. Now since you mention it, I remember with absolute assurance thinking when I wrote that, How ironic it is that we should think events and specific exterior achievements should be the means by which man's nature is fathomed. Without knowing, and in a sense without really having adequate reason to feel so, I was absolutely confident— and this remained to be proved—that in Brady's emotionally muted relationships and in his failure to relate to others there was the drama, however submerged, of much American life.

BOOTH: But as far as you can remember, you hadn't at that moment planned to show him not only with a muted emotional life but with this rich imaginative gift which can yield his visions? I hadn't really realized until this last reading the full extent of his visionary experience, how close he comes by the end to being able to see the world of suffering humanity in a really penetrating way.

MORRIS: Let us say that I must have been convinced of that in a fashion—and then the proof awaited. The first readers of the book, in 1951 when it was published, were uniformly disturbed by the fact that any writer should spend so much time and so much concern on a man with so much of his life left out. They did not feel the concern that the author felt.

BOOTH: Uniformly?

MORRIS: Oh, yes. Well, there were two or three rather fanatically favorable reviews from the backwoods. One from Oklahoma: the man was almost hysterically sympathetic. But in the main all the eastern reviews were essentially negative. They were polite on one or two occasions but basically negative. A magazine like *Time*, which gave it a few lines, had only to say that I had seemed to be unaware that in imitating Sherwood Anderson's *Triumph of the Egg* I was really not making much of a contribution to fiction. The irony is, at that point I had not read *The Triumph of the Egg*. And perhaps a good thing—otherwise I might have been self-conscious about making Brady a butter-and-egg man. I would have said, "O my God! No."

This type of unconscious plagiarism must occur in American writing repeatedly. It's rather good in a way that a beginning writer be unread and unlettered; otherwise, he would have even greater inhibitions than he has.

BOOTH: Pursuing my point from another angle: When you began, did you have the Santa Claus episode in mind, or did that come as you were writing?

MORRIS: The Santa Claus role is of interest. I hadn't had such a twist remotely in mind. What interests me is how this remote, unseen, possibility would come to pass as if inevitable. At the end of his wandering, seemingly aimless, life, Brady should fall into the persona most appropriate to him. It has the rightness about it that life seldom has, and I find it hard to imagine another convincing resolution. I did not want him fading, like a voice, into the background. However, his stumbling on this guise was not an accident.

The Santa Claus role also derives from the attention that I gave Santa Claus as a boy, and the lack of attention he occasionally gave me. Perhaps the clue is in the *lack* of attention, there being more pathos in it.

For example, when I was living with the Irish family in Omaha I had one memorable Christmas. My father was having difficulties with his marital life, among other things, and months might pass before I saw him. So I was anxious to convince the Mulligans that my father still loved me. I saved up money, made by selling papers, and bought myself a pawned gold watch—the case could be unscrewed, and the works examined—and then I wrapped this watch in a series of boxes, each one larger than the previous—you see we have here an embryo fiction writer—and gave this larger carton to myself at Christmas, with love from my father. There it was under the tree on Christmas morning. I do have a vague but palpable sense of guilt that I *enjoyed* the pathos of it. In this way writers are made, not born.

One further experience. My first job in Chicago, as I mentioned, was in the Montgomery Ward warehouse on Canal Street, where during the Christmas rush I was taken off my regular job to blow balloons for Santa Claus in the toy department. I sat concealed behind him, handing up the balloons as I blew them. You will agree that's a very memorable thing for a boy to be *paid* to do.

Both of these scenes are full of pathos, a pathos that is appropriate to Brady's nature. I think of pathos as very American. It is really the music or the syrup in which we have our existence. To get out of it or above it is extremely rare; when we fall below it, we fall into something that is bathetic rather than pathetic.

BOOTH: I am struck by how greatly transformed all this experience becomes in the finished product. The pathos of the little boy wishing his father would be Santa Claus gets turned into the pathos of the old man who can *become* Santa Claus. The boy who was you actually passing out balloons beneath Santa Claus's feet gets transformed into a half-wit doing the same thing. (I wouldn't want to make too much of that, your secret view of yourself as a half-wit passing out balloons!) But what strikes me is that in your account so far there is nothing to explain your turning Brady into more than just a Santa Claus: you turn him into a Santa Claus who is able to imagine like an artist. In fact, you turn him *into* an artist—an inarticulate artist who has only thoughts not words. Where does all that come from—out of your adult interest in how worlds get themselves created?

MORRIS: Well, it must. I cannot attempt to go back to what I might have been feeling rather than what I was motivated by during the early drafts of *The Works of Love*. It was expanding rather freely, but up until the Chicago incident the book was still pretty much as we find it now. The expansions did not occur until I was faced with the resolution of Brady's life as an adult. Should his life simply come to an end as we have it in the book, or should he have recurring experiences?

I was a country boy when we moved to Chicago, but in a few years time I had "seen" a good deal of life. Most of my living was done in the YMCA at Larrabee Street and Blackhawk, soon to be known as "Death's corner." My actual experience was that of a boy, and limited, but the city charged and fertilized my imagination. Twenty years later, pondering the life of Brady, I stayed within the physical scope of my limited experience, but expanded freely on Brady's life in *my* world. In the late forties I had "discovered" Sherwood Anderson, and found in his muted, groping characters the confirmation of my feelings about Will Brady. This acknowledgment is made at the front of the book. Writing within the tonal range I had established I could sense what seemed plausible for Brady, or implausible.

BOOTH: Well, that all makes marvelous sense, but you keep dodging my questions about those visions. And I do want to keep pushing you about them because not only do these episodes occur, but this man stands at his window and looks out and has experiences that are quantitatively the text of the whole novel; there is more time spent on his silent wonder about the world and figuring it out than on any other single thing.

Let me put the question quite precisely. Somewhere along the line you discovered that the Santa Claus episode is going to be your climax. Did you then have to go back through and pack in preparation for that climax? Had you by that time decided also to show him having a vision of the shore of Lake Michigan and of the people walking into the lake? Was that something that came later or did it come earlier? And if it came later, did you then have to go back and insert other visions like that in the earlier parts of the novel, or had they been there all the while?

MORRIS: No, they had been there. It was all there, as we now find it, up to and through the sun lamp. After the sun lamp I greatly expanded on Brady's life—in the manner of a dreamer made new by the lamp—and he had a series of adventures with women, a sort of *Bildungsroman* of the life that begins after forty. All of it comical.

There were some good scenes, but both Brady and the reader were lost. You will find some of it in the short fiction. The writer was also lost, and he put the book aside for about two years. Thanks to that I was able to fearlessly cut it back to where we now find it.

Over one long hot summer and fall I helped my father sort his freight waybills in the tower room. He did this at night, and I would help him until one or two o'clock in the morning. Then I would eat at one of the all-night Thompson's restaurants, of the sort that pile grapefruit in their windows, then begin the long, wondrous walk that took me up Michigan Avenue to the lake front, the sand at Oak Street beach trampled but empty, the green light of dawn reflected in the windows of the Gold Coast apartments, the green-guttered homes of the rich, with perhaps one or two of the handsome men and the beautiful women out for an early morning ride on the bridle path—but you see I am remembering what I have written, or at least what I experienced, through the eyes of Brady. I was there, but it is now through his eyes that I see it. Is that a kind of poetic justice? The sense of the sleeping city, humming like a power plant, overwhelmed me. I will never be free of these impressions. I was responding to Chicago like a dreaming boy who antici- pates the life and experiences of manhood, the promise of wealth, adventure, and beautiful women. I think we can say that Will Brady's dreams were not substantially different than mine.

BOOTH: At that time you had no remote idea of be- coming a writer yourself? You weren't thinking, "I am having a rich, imaginative experience, which will some- time be useful to me when I become a writer"? That was all far in the future?

MORRIS: I did not know such books, or such writers existed. I assumed they came with libraries, like paintings came with museums. And I think I gained more than I lost. It is what the writer experiences before he knows he is *having* an experience that is important. *These* impressions are inexhaustible. The others are real enough, but he can be free of them. The naive experience has the freshness of creation about it. You don't learn from it, and you don't replace it. Chicago provided me with such an experience, and it found its reflection in Brady. Does that seem strange? On the evidence, it is true to the imagination. I remember how astonished I was to find, in my last year in high school, a book written by a man who was *alive*, about the lives and thoughts living people were having.

BOOTH: How old were you? About eighteen?

MORRIS: Yes, eighteen, nineteen. Now I remember something. All through high school I was gripped with a passion for drawing. I have a very small talent, but God how I worked at it. I dreamed of being a political cartoonist, like those seen on the front pages of newspapers. I did not associate drawing with painting, or the history of art I was studying, as the student would today. I now see that this obsessive concern may well have diverted me from other interests. I slaved at it. It came as natural to me as Horatio Alger.

BOOTH: And are you really saying—it does seem almost incredible considering the lives of most other novelists—that by the age of eighteen or nineteen you had never tried to write any stories, any poems? And you had kept no journals? Are you sure, or is this something you are repressing?

MORRIS: Well, since you force my hand, I am able to record the moment in the seventh year of my elementary school in Omaha when we were told or invited to write a poem; and I met this occasion with typical audacity. I wrote several pages of something that went . . . well, it went like this:

> The lake was quite a ways away
> And Willy was quite tired
> When he reached the rough and muddy shore
> Of the lake he oft admired.

Now it went on like that, if you can believe it, for about three pages.

BOOTH: But the hero *was* named Willy?

MORRIS: The hero *was* named Willy, which is of interest when you think of Will and Willy Brady. Now the lake was right down on the corner. It was in what was called Turner Park at that time, just a block down. But it is of interest that a certain facility in language must have been evident since I turned out three pages of this sort of thing on demand.

Why I remember it, I am not quite sure. The remarkably bad "poetry" is often unforgettable.

BOOTH: But you kept no journal through all that time?

MORRIS: The very concept of a journal would have blown my mind! It's perfectly true that journals are possible to sophisticated youngsters today, and they were then, to those whose families had an education or had some home background in which a little reading was done. All through American literature we find children who were both precocious and sophisticated. But in my experience in the Midwest *un*consciousness like mine was very common.

BOOTH: It is *not* common for productive authors to have no experience of writing before they are nineteen. That's very unusual.

MORRIS: It probably is. I was simply too preoccupied with living—no, not with living exactly, but with being lived. You know, if I had been sitting at home, like many less active youngsters, reading because I had time, and thinking about what I was reading, I might have been writing. I had this facility, obviously, and it was encouraged in high school, but I didn't know what the encouragement meant. In another environment, I would have made a few stumbling efforts to write.

BOOTH: But by the time you published your first novel you had done a good deal of reading and thinking about writing?

MORRIS: I was still naive about what we would think of as an intelligent or informed approach to writing fiction. I lacked experience reading it. I did not lack, let's say, a certain kind of educated response to writing. I'd done a lot of reading in college, but none of it had been contemporary, and very little of my reading until my last year had been with the idea that I might be learning from it. In fact, the idea that I could learn about writing from reading did not come until the middle of the forties, largely because the notion of contemporary literature as a subject available to young people for study is really quite recent. I didn't feel deprived.

I can remember the first time I saw on a reading shelf at college a copy of *This Side of Paradise*. And I picked up that book and took it on a weekend down to Balboa and read it there with two or three friends. I was impressed by it, but I have no feeling that the quality of that impression was permanent. I was simply aware that I had come upon what we would call a work of literature. I knew it was an imaginative reconstruction of a life that was near to me. This fascinated me without any question, but I was much too green to sense *why* it fascinated me or think that I might do it.

BOOTH: But you must have read a great deal in high school, even if not contemporary writing. Yet it never occurred to you, you say, to think how differently you were doing the thing from the way Fitzgerald did it, or that your processes might be different from Henry Fielding's or Nathaniel Hawthorne's?

MORRIS: You'll have to take my word for it. I had no knowledge of it, time for it, nor interest in it, until I had written several books. I assumed one learned to write by writing, wisdom I had picked up somewhere. Predictably, I was a slow learner. What we call a good but untrained voice. The breakthrough occurred with *My Uncle Dudley*, written in five or six weeks in Los Angeles. I was making a photographic tour of the country, and had stopped there before heading back east. The book grew out of a surge of memories about the past—I had been in L.A. as a boy, in 1926 or '27—and the intervening years provided the perspective I needed. The long apprenticeship of writing I had put in seemed to have waited on that occasion. The book flowed. Uncle Dudley is seen with both sympathy and detachment, through the boy's eyes.

BOOTH: But you *had* read *Huckleberry Finn*?

MORRIS: As a boy in grade school. As a matter of fact, I *was* Huck Finn in one of those Parent Day entertainments. In 1940 I had still not read the book as a *writer*. Another six or seven years pass before that happens, and I sense to what extent it had shaped my own language. Let's say that I had come along at a time when the vernacular was making writers, rather than writers making vernacular.

BOOTH: By the time you came to write *The Works of Love* some seven or eight years later, you still worked organically, I gather, though you were much more knowledgeable in the craft of fiction?

MORRIS: Yes and no. I proved to be crafty enough for the small scale, uncomplicated volume, but I was untried when I got into the reaches of Brady. I had no detachment. I gave myself entirely to what I was writing, what I proved to be imagining. That gave the writing tone and substance, but it smothered the book. I recall considerable highfalutin tampering, in which I hoped poetic titles would clarify my purpose. They did not. Only bold surgery would save the patient, and that was what he got.

It's interesting to me that a younger man, at the start of his career, should become so profoundly involved with an older man nearing the end of the line. On reflection it proves that this is not unusual. It constitutes a special challenge to the man and the writer. Take Joyce, for example, dealing with Gabriel Conroy in "The Dead." Joyce is only twenty-six, living in exile in Trieste, and in coming to terms with the older man he is shaping the terms of his own consciousness. Gabriel is that ideal projection of the man, and the lover, who manages to come to terms with himself, pitiful as he believes himself to be. I see that this is also true of Brady. Dealing with the older man releases in the writer the affection, longing, and wonder they may not feel for themselves, or their contemporaries. Thomas Mann, at thirty-six, re-creates Tonio Kröger, and a marvelous thing happens: along the way he senses the need for Gustave Aschenbach, who will appear in *Death in Venice*. All the way through *Tonio Kröger* Mann is looking forward to Aschenbach, the *achieved* artist, who is soon to have his composure shattered. Thinking about somebody older, rather than somebody younger, releases special sympathies in the imagination—sympathies that lie with the future, rather than the past. We have this same thing happening with Tolstoy and Ivan Ilyich, but at a moment when Tolstoy is in crisis. To redeem himself he must do away with Ilyich.

BOOTH: Does this mean that you have had more difficulty with the characters who are closest to you, like Boyd in *The Field of Vision* and *Ceremony in Lone Tree,* than you have had with characters that are more remote?

MORRIS: Right on the nose. I think of it less as a difficulty than a dissatisfaction. Boyd does not satisfy me, and I often wonder why. Do I have an answer when I say he is too *close* to the author? Especially in time. The same problem exists with Webb in *The Deep Sleep.* He is too much of a spokesman. Boyd has umbilical problems. He is not a separate creation.

BOOTH: Have you killed him off?

MORRIS: Yes. Nor do I hear him complaining, like Hamlet's ghost.

BOOTH: At various times you have experimented with other characters who, like Boyd, in some way resemble the author; or you have invented characters like Lehman in *The Field of Vision* who can speak a kind of wisdom as a background of norms for the other characters. In recent novels you tend to eliminate such voices. Is this because you find that you can get the evaluations you want without this overt talk? Or is it that you think the world, because of the body of your work, is now beginning to know the sort of context in which to read it?

MORRIS: Certainly not that the world has learned to read me—what world is that? The change does interest me, however. For instance, I now find it hard to understand the great enthusiasm I brought to the multiple-voice fiction I was once so fond of. Such as in *The Field of Vision* and *The Deep Sleep*, continuing into *Ceremony.* It seemed to me that these many voices was my own appropriate voice. Why should I speak for them? Let them speak for themselves—and when the writing is good, this is *not* an illusion. Then it tapers off, like a romance. *One Day* would appear to be its full-throated swan song. I suppose that every new way of working impresses the writer with its possibilities, more than its limitations. Then he comes to recognize its limitations. When that recognition is full and assured he moves on to something else, or he stops writing. Or shall we say that he should stop writing.

After almost thirty-five years of fiction writing I see that some of my work is now exterior to me. It might almost have been written by somebody else. It is not a rejection, but a full acceptance. I am baffled by Ignazio Silone *rewriting* his *Bread and Wine* after almost thirty years: bringing it up to date. Would you like to do that with your family? They either exist in their own time and place, or they have no authentic existence. It defines him as a nonfiction writer, not fully aware of what he is doing. In the same breath, he damned what he had once done.

We know that the personality which we think of as "you" and "I" have is merely a social surrogate for another self that goes about its appropriate business, and that seems to be—and I think really is—a much more civilized personality than the one we have to make do with. But I believe this personality, for those who can indulge it—that is, those who can give it the attention that the writer gives it, the writer who is always in a kind of dialogue with it—makes fiction as flowers come on plants and leaves on bushes. It is a natural outgrowth of a need that otherwise is not gratified. The simpler forms of life take care of this need on a simpler level. Being more complex, man has to work out a means by which he is able to respond to his environment, not simply as an adaptive gesture but as a creative gesture.

BOOTH: With this concept of fiction as a natural organic growth on the life of man and your own novel as a kind of natural organic growth from your life, you can't, then *choose* a new or a particular technique? Rather, the technique chooses you at a given time. This is also true, I take it, for the subject matter. You can't make an arbitrary choice: *Now* I am going to do a Nebraska novel again; or, *now* I am not going to do a Nebraska novel again.

MORRIS: That's a good point, Wayne. Recently a reader, a teacher out at Central City or Kearney or somewhere, came up to me and said, "Oh, when are you going to finish the trilogy? When are you going to finish the trilogy?" She had picked up the idea, as reviewers do, that if you do two books, there has to be three. I think many readers jump to this conclusion. It's good that we don't have the idea of fives—imagine how much more bad fiction there would be! The expectation that there had to be another book about Boyd was conveyed to me after *Ceremony in Lone Tree* by many readers. In *another* book, surely the so-called loose ends could be brought together.

There *is* a kind of writer who is good at this. Perhaps they are not of the first rank: I think of all the novels that Mazo de la Roche wrote about the Whiteoaks of Jalna and the not-so-Whiteoaks of Jalna. Such continuation is of course very gratifying to readers who hang in there. See what Galsworthy did with the Forsyte family.

But come back to that other kind of fiction, in which the author himself is involved with his works, not merely in writing something for other people but in writing what seems to be necessary to his conscious existence, to his sense of well-being. For such a writer, when he finishes with something, he *finishes* with it; he is not left with continuations that he can go on knitting until he runs out of yarn.

This conceit reflects my own experience as a writer, relying on the sap that keeps rising, the force that drives the flower, as Dylan Thomas put it. It is plantlike. We put it in the sun and when it doesn't grow, we take it and put it in another room. I don't think of repotting the plant. The plant must make its own way.

BOOTH: I like the organic metaphor, but I keep wanting to come back to particular cases to see how you actually work, in literal detail. Even the organic novelist obviously still has the matter of collecting notes, starting a novel, having it fail to go. Let me put a simple question, and move out from there. How many actual novels, whether they ever reach fiction or not, do you have "growing" at a given time?

MORRIS: You don't mean simultaneously?

BOOTH: I mean actual notes that exist in some kind of manuscript form, starts on a novel, something you are actually working on.

MORRIS: It is so unusual for me to have more than one or two things in mind at once that I don't find this a fruitful question.

BOOTH: You've answered my question. You don't have a collection of possibilities.

MORRIS: Recently, within the last three or four years, I have been able to think of two or three simultaneous activities. That is, for the first time in my life I have been able to turn from one work to another. In the main this has been from fiction to nonfiction, but I have also turned from fiction to fiction. In the past, which we have been basically concerned with, my preoccupation with what I was doing was always complete.

I've always been amazed, absolutely staggered, to learn that there are people who have the craft of fiction so available to them that they can keep two or three books going at the same time. When one book grows a little slack, they turn over to another. And some are good writers. I don't think of them as writers who will mean the most to me, but they are good writers.

I can now grasp this facility, but I could not practice it because I would almost feel as if in turning away from a book, I was cheating the people in the book of the attention that they really deserve. It's a little bit like sharing too many friends at a single moment. If you want to give your attention to the friends who are there, you do not suddenly go to the door and ask in another roomful.

BOOTH: Do you ever start a book, lay it aside, and some ten years later come back to it?

MORRIS: I have started books that prove to have short circuits, and seem to profit from long incubation. I have books that are long, and fail to incubate. They grew out of my obsession with an experience that simply lacked fictive substance. My winter at Schloss Ranna, in Austria, for example. I will never fully recover from it. The best I have managed to do is the Time Past section in *Cause for Wonder*. I wrote several long manuscripts in the late thirties. I tried it again just a few years ago. A case of impure infatuation. I do not, alas, give adequate thought to what the cumulative effects of books might be, or whether there *is* a cumulative effect. They constitute, for me, a chain of being, and I find my being by going from one to the other.

BOOTH: That lack of calculation in your work is shown in a variety of ways. You haven't been a good publicist for your work—you are not, in my view, someone who is good at capitalizing on yourself publicly. You haven't given attention to what so many novelists spend a great deal of time working on—how to make your fame, not by writing, but by calculating what to write, and by being "a writer."

II

BOOTH: We've talked about the way in which you see your imagination transforming materials from life, and we have talked about individual characters, but we have not talked about categories of characters. We could talk about fathers, we could talk about sons, we could talk about daughters, and so on. I would like to consider one of the big categories that I have heard some of your readers worry about, namely women, and then we could turn to particular female characters. I've heard somebody say that you have never fully portrayed a sympathetic woman. Yours are always somehow caricatured or diminished. I think this is not true, but I would like to have your response.

MORRIS: The question poses my relationship to fiction from a fresh perspective. At no time have I ever calculated my position in regard to women or men or anything else. What we have is something that comes straight from me with my defenses down. A woman will appear in the early fiction and I don't believe I would have any more attitude toward her role there than I would if a dog would appear. . . . That's an unfortunate metaphor, but—

BOOTH: You would say the same thing about a man.

MORRIS: Of course, or even more. Let's see if we can refocus on it with reference to specific characters. There is no woman of any consequence in *My Uncle Dudley*. There is just the mention of a couple of women as objects of interest to the old man and little flashes of interest in feminine beauty and this sort of thing.

BOOTH: There is the one fine conversation between Dudley and the woman he talks with on the porch. There he finds a woman he appreciates and whom we appreciate as a real character.

MORRIS: But she is also very much "a character." She derives from the boy's imagining the sort of woman that Dudley would have imagined, and then he puts her into this situation. So we have a fantasy twice removed from reality—but that's part of the farcical tone of *Dudley,* so it is all right. Then in *The Man Who Was There,* we have the first appearance of a series of grandmothers. The young people are going west, and the grandmother goes along with them.

BOOTH: She goes with Private Reagan, and she dies out there.

MORRIS: We get a series of women, older people, who are on the verge of being comical caricatures, all of whom attend Private Reagan's funeral. And they are handled sometimes broadly and sometimes with a touch of acid. The narration is largely carried on in the third person. The fiction was rather skillfully contrived, considering my inexperience at the time. In fact that entire section called "Private Reagan" was a separate piece of fiction, about fifty or sixty pages long, which came very near being published as a story. It reveals my attitude as a young man toward men and women no longer young. They are comical, but not grotesque. The caricature is characteristically American: we might say vernacular. I think both Twain and Ring Lardner might have enjoyed it. The writer was fascinated by the comedy on the surface, and is not at all disturbed by what he fails to see. A blissful state of ignorance.

BOOTH: So you're saying that your attitude toward the grandmother was not particularly a matter of her being a woman but that she was of the older generation?

MORRIS: I think so. I am seeing them as amusing distortions, superficially experienced and insuffiiciently known. In *The Man Who Was There* most of the women are in-laws and relations taken hot and simmering off the griddle, recently observed. Private Reagan, however, is a whole cloth piece of fiction, having no parallel in my experience. He is the first of the "possessed" characters, like Hyman Kopfman, toward which I am powerfully drawn. I remember I was very much taken by the charm and sweetness of Annie Mae, the retarded child of Adelaide. I see in all of this now, as I did not then, something of the grotesquerie of *Pudd'nhead Wilson*. We are still a crazy lot.

BOOTH: You seem in fact to have judged the other characters, in part, according to whether they can deal with her as a person or treat her merely as a category?

MORRIS: That's probably right. I've never thought of it in that light, but I think it's true. I was seeing them, screening them, through the eyes of the child.

BOOTH: Consider the women in *The Works of Love*. Except for Anna Mason there are really no strongly sympathetic women there. Somebody could say you are antifeminist. But there are no sympathetic males there either, in the sense of being fully admirable. The strongest single person in the book is Anna Mason.

MORRIS: Wayne, I'm ceaselessly mystified by sophisticated readers who feel compelled to simplify, to fumigate, to classify, rather than *accept* the character. I am astonished to learn that a *Morris* reader would find the women in *The Works of Love* unsympathetically portrayed. I bled for them. I felt deeply for them. Ethel Bassett is powerfully strange, but she is not unattractive. Gertrude is Gertrude: you'll find her standing in line at any recent movie. And Mrs. Plinski? I love Mrs. Plinski. People *are* indeed strange, and some of them are women.

BOOTH: I don't think readers worry so much about whether they are sympathetically *portrayed*—there is, after all, a kind of endemic sympathy for all your characters in all your books. The question is whether there are any fully mature, coping women. Now we mentioned that Anna Mason *is* a giant of a human being. But in rereading *The Works of Love* this time, I could see why careless readers would find her overshadowed by some of the other women, especially that chain of people who answer Brady's ad. The harridans that you assemble there make really quite a remarkable, wonderfully funny, and terrifying list. You could have had Will Brady meet women who would have fully responded to him. Will Brady never does. And that seems to some readers to imply that there are no women out there who could.

MORRIS: It is Brady's nature to meet the women he met, not a sampling from the Bureau of Good House-keeping. Readers looking for such types are not fiction readers. Curiously enough, a good part of the manuscript that was cut concerned itself with women sympathetic to Brady, however strange. There is a story called "The Lover," another called "Magic." The woman in this story is nothing but a voice, yet she anticipates the *ewige weibliche* figures that appear later. Mrs. Erskine, in *The Deep Sleep*, and that powerhouse in *One Day*. What was the name of that woman?

BOOTH: In real life?

MORRIS: No, in the fiction. Evelina! In any case, there is in my imagination a conceptual, fictive Eve. She is a figure that is recurrent and that appears, in one draft, at the end of Brady's life but she is not in the book published. Although she is uniquely American—we don't have a parallel for her anywhere—this "basic" woman is represented in the European female as a kind of mixture of Gertrude Stein and Alma Mahler, if you can imagine!

She has extraordinary attraction and assurance; she is "woman" in the mythic sense of the word, and very close to caricature, as such a figure often is. She embodies a certain unpredictableness of temper, a rather ridiculous eccentricity, but she is basically a product of man defaulting in his role as man. The woman is left having to be two personalities in order to replace what the man has failed to provide.

Most women fail to do this. Mrs. Porter in *The Deep Sleep* is in a quandary as to what to do because she has no subtlety in her nature. She does what she can, the Judge having defaulted. But these other women are the result of a positive but almost comical effort to adjust to an impossible situation. They are very close to the "You men!" cry of vaudeville and farce.

BOOTH: It is clear that you have tried to transcend the ordinary categorizations we make—women, men, old people, young people. But I am still interested to know whether you've ever been tempted to dramatize at length someone like Anna Mason, the strong, generous, firm-footed, successful woman?

MORRIS: Well . . .

BOOTH: Or man, for that matter. It's really not the woman question at all. None of your characters are as firmly planted in life as you yourself are.

MORRIS: Yes, I think some are. Parsons and Webb, McKee and Foley; also Cowie lives in this world, insofar as it seems livable. I think of the character who appears in various guises as the Texan and later ends up in *A Life*. He is firmly planted, at least as we come to know him in *A Life*. He is as plantlike in the society as an aware man can be who has rejected—or has never experienced—a great deal of sophistication and has no hunger for it. He is satisfied in the world he lives in.

But let's go back to an effort to present women, or woman, on a more acceptable plane, in *Ceremony in Lone Tree*. Now, I think Mrs. McKee is, or comes close to being, representative of a positive but essentially trapped woman, one whose nature remains entirely feminine and who yet within a circumscribed area attempts to be a full person. At no time is she caricatured. That is, I feel she suffers without comic redemption. She isn't suddenly made to be agreeable just because she is growing old and is shuffled around. I feel toward her a rather consistent poignancy and sympathy. Since she must be McKee's wife, we have the dilemma: she must be shaped essentially by sentiments that shaped the people of Willa Cather. Into her world impinges Boyd, who is a little bit like a Nebraska Gatsby in his sophistication. He has been shaped by the same "dreams." They have a confrontation that is as romantically extreme as that experienced by Zelda and Fitzgerald. Each is essentially in love with love, and with romance.

BOOTH: Boyd is in love with his romantic self.

MORRIS: Right, and also in love with the "idea" of such a woman as Mrs. McKee was at that time. Lois I called her. An attractive woman, very cool for the period, looking very good when she dressed up, waiting for the moment to fulfill itself to which she was the ornament. A woman of her period. She could fit right into Fitzgerald. And Boyd is a Fitzgerald offshoot in this sense; he attempts to walk on water rather than settle matters at West Egg like Gatsby.

But I do tend to think of Mrs. McKee primarily in her relationship with McKee: of these two people, I feel that McKee is more fully conscious than Mrs. McKee. Do you feel that way yourself?

BOOTH: Yes, I do. We see her more often from the outside, even though you do give her her chapters.

MORRIS: In *The Field of Vision* we see her as essentially a frustrated woman who is, in a sense, the narrator. The story seemed to be using her for the purposes of the story.

BOOTH: In *Ceremony* you start getting closer and closer to her; and by the end, one feels there is a ceremony of reconciliation with her as with almost all the characters. We have got far inside them. This is especially true of Lois, after the satirical use of her in *The Field of Vision*. We find a full reconciliation with her, but still she is a maimed woman.

MORRIS: That is the right word: maimed. You suggest that all the characters achieve essentially a kind of reconciliation. Insofar as there is a shaping, coherent motivation on my part, in that book, that is it.

BOOTH: Do you want to drop the woman question?

MORRIS: Let us admit that in general the reader is going to feel that the women in my fiction are maimed and are more victimized than the men. Yet the men, too, are often victims. One would think that I would weary of this, and that I would take up as a novelty the idea of other types of women. I think we have some evidence that this happened. There is Lou Baker, as well as Foley, in *The Huge Season*. I feel Foley is a notch above Boyd, in achieving his own nature. The opinions readers have about *fictions* reveal the illusions they hold about themselves—a privately indulged fiction.

I must again admit my willingness to be preoccupied with what I *find* next on my agenda, rather than what I have planned, or projected. The new work grows from the old. Wasn't it Stendhal who said, "I wake up in the morning and I see what is written on the pad before me"? Too much of my fiction is of this sort; perhaps I don't spend enough time thinking during the night! I wake up and find something on the pad before me.

But think of the younger women who have appeared in my fiction. They represent a new breed. We get a couple of them in *Ceremony*. There's the one that Boyd picks up in Nevada. She comes back with him and is something of a trial run for Chickpea in *One Day*. Then consider the young woman in *What a Way to Go*. She is a further development of Sweet Jesus in *Ceremony*. Would you say these *jeunes filles* are romantically conceived? They seem almost unrelated to their adult environment. They make a new start. Today we would say liberated. How about Lou Baker in *The Huge Season*? The seed is always there, but the times are out of joint. There is nothing in any of the other people in *One Day* that can compare with Chickpea—she is the most open, experiences the most that is contemporary; and she is a foil to the most sympathetic of the male characters, Cowie.

Do we find a duality in my fiction? The older women are essentially idealized, rather mythically scaled figures who bluster through their novels, largely filling the gaps left by their weak men. At the bottom of the scale there is a younger generation, young women attempting to appear and take their place. In *One Day* we have a relatively sophisticated environment, so Chickpea is a different young woman. But the two have the same audacity.

In short, I am shifting over to the female some of the audacity that seemed to be wasted on the males. I am becoming more sympathetic with the new than I was with the old. There is no male character who now appears to be sharing this quality of audacity. My fiction seems to be changing. Again.

BOOTH: It will bear watching.

"The Dictates of Style"

A CONVERSATION BETWEEN
DAVID MADDEN AND WRIGHT MORRIS

Every writer who is sufficiently self-aware to
know what he is doing, and how he does it,
sooner or later is confronted with the dictates
of style. If he *has* a style, it is the style that
dictates what he says. *What* he says, of course,
is how he says it.

Wright Morris, *The Territory Ahead*

David Madden took the occasion of his visit to Wright
Morris on the campus of the University of Nebraska–
Lincoln to reconsider all his published comments on
style, drawing on his periodical essays, textbooks, and
encyclopedia articles. Some of his conclusions about
Morris's style he has expressed in eighteen published
essays and his book *Wright Morris* (1964), the only
full-length study of Morris to date.

Madden has repeatedly considered the major problems
to which Morris's style gives rise. Acknowledging that
the novels make unusual demands on the reader, he has
noted that through all the published novels Morris
refines a unique style, deliberately transforming stock
characterization, trite situation, and schematic narrative through language revivified by fresh response. He
has stated in his critical studies that for Morris "character is revealed cliché," the characters being unable to
experience the present until they have come to terms
with triteness.

The result is what Madden has called a "rhetoric of meditation" which modulates between the vernacular and formal syntax. Eliminating or minimizing conventional kinds of action, Morris presents moments of perception that in themselves create dramatic action. Madden has observed that Morris adapts to his fiction stylistic devices of both poetry and expository discourse: patterned syntax, Jamesian parenthesis, rhetorical questioning, punning, paradox, metaphor, and always humor. Throughout the books one finds careful variations of tone, sentence by sentence, paragraph by paragraph, even word by word, which require close scrutiny to be fully appreciated.

In conversations David Madden and Wright Morris discussed "the dictates of style," as that style has been analyzed by Madden and other critics.

MADDEN: In my view you're one of the most careful stylists in American fiction today. Every sentence, every word, seems to be weighed for its maximum effect. I imagine that you refine and hone the language with constant revisions. Do you revise line by line as you go along, or do you go back after a novel is pretty well finished and recast phrases, sentences, paragraphs into their most effective positions? Do you correct your first drafts before or after first writing?

MORRIS: Neither.

MADDEN: You mean that you *don't* revise? But if you don't rewrite, how do you achieve this elaborate and complicated style the first time around?

MORRIS: Nothing is ever "the first time around." After the first experiments, it's the fourth time around, or the seventh, or the twelfth—finally, with these latest books, it's the twenty-first or twenty-second time around, even though I'm just writing them for the first time. At this late date I adapt a new style rather easily when I respond to a new fictive situation. My revisions were all done many years ago.

Let's consider, to be explicit, the boy in *Fire Sermon*. The boy's voice more than the old man's is used for the center of interest in that novel. The author speaks through the boy more than through the old man—the old man is peripheral in that book, though he is central in the next book, *A Life*. *Fire Sermon* began with an image of this old geezer in his neon-flaming, cross-cornered hat, holding that sign, the coat too big for him. He was out there in front of the school, the kids teasing him all the time. He was a comical figure in a sense. Well, the moment I had that, I had something that appealed to me. I didn't know what I was going to do with it, but I began to be interested in possibilities that I had not entertained for years—a boy and an old man as subject for a piece of fiction.

The reason that this came about is a complexity that we don't have to go into now. It was full cycle in a sense, for this situation is like that in *My Uncle Dudley*, my first novel published thirty-five years ago. Only the situation is in reverse. I hit on the idea that the tone was going to be essentially out of the boy, that we were going to see this experience in the main filtered through his nature, rather than the old man's. On a card (usually it's on a card because there's always something in the typewriter) I wrote two or three sentences, and when I went back to my study with these three sentences and managed to type them out, I began to add others. Ordinarily when I reach the point of writing down three or four sentences, I am attentive to the tone of the passage as well as to the nature of the particular character who speaks or thinks. After that it is mostly a question of going on. One paragraph, the first few paragraphs, may require a little shaping afterwards—I may get a little too much information in, so I have to strike out things. But mostly I simply proceed, continuing what I have originally set down.

All of *Fire Sermon* was relatively unchanged from its first draft, as I think the manuscript will attest. You would find one or two passages with little problems of emphasis and timing, like the farmhouse just before the fire. You might find a reconsideration of the number and way the events occurred in the cemetery. There might be a question, on the trip back, of whether one incident is allowed to appear in a certain scene or in another, like the incident of the car in the street when the old man is asked what he wants for it, or the incident of that man and his wife in the trailer, or the incident of the sheep crossing the road. But the manuscript, I think, will testify that these changes have nothing to do with the refinements of style. The style came naturally.

MADDEN: When I try to analyze your style in terms of diction, syntax, grammatical structure, interpolation, parenthetical delays, rhythm, your use of prepositions, sentence fragments, rhetorical questions, and parallel structure, I never would assume that these came without fifty changes. Is the stylistic method of these late books characteristic of the earlier books?

MORRIS: No. This is what we need to keep in perspective. I was very ignorant as well as very naive when I began, but my first writing gave some evidence of a facility for language. They give rather early evidence of a preoccupation with using language in the most economical way possible. These early pieces were really epiphanies.

MADDEN: Had you read Joyce?

MORRIS: No, I had read no Joyce.

MADDEN: You mean you hit on epiphanies by yourself?

MORRIS: I hit on the epiphany because it was a way of putting into a small statement the essence of an experience. In my use of language there is an element that the narrative novelist has no interest in, might even find obstructive. He would say, One of the things that is wrong with this novel is that it holds the reader up. He has to read too carefully. I would agree. But that's the way I write. When I put a paragraph together, if it doesn't have a kind of poetic substance, I think it's really not of much interest.

MADDEN: Did you rework then as you went along, the way one would rework separate poems?

MORRIS: All of my apprentice writing—five long years of it—showed a preoccupation with cadence and rhythm. In the late thirties it became obsessive and stifling. The last draft of a long novel has the hypnotic cadence of a breathing exercise. It needs to be *canted*—read with the lips. Here is the opening sentence, after more than forty years!

Snow be-gan to fall on Schot-ten-gas-see.

I combined this with an economy that occasionally defied comprehension. I *implied* everything. I broke out of this bind, in 1940, by turning from writing to photography, and a long photo-collecting tour of most of the country. This breather broke the spell I had worked myself into, but it did not modify my passion for economy. When I began to write again—I was midway on the tour—I was free of both the previous subject and the manner, and experienced a life-enhancing release. The book was *My Uncle Dudley*. The voice was that of the boy I had been in the mid-twenties. The pacing, cadence, rhythm dam was broken, but I held fast to the economy.

MADDEN: In your later writing, which you're saying is different, you give to every sentence, to every detail, an equal ring of authority. The uniformity runs the risk of exhausting the reader. He responds to everything as if everything is equally important.

MORRIS: I'm open to this criticism. As I shape the sentence on the page it seems to me that everything *is* equal. Gertrude Stein came to this practice through observation. She saw it was what Cézanne was up to in his painting. So we have the ceaseless *Making of Americans*. The insight is profound, but in actual practice we can *look* at the painting, as a painting, but *The Making of Americans* must be read, and read, and reread. A ten-minute *look* is a long time. The novel takes a week, and part of its effect is instant erasure of what we have just read. In my own practice I eliminate "the pause that refreshes," so common to the older fiction. My idea of relevance is somewhat rarefied. There's very little chance for the reader to relax.

MADDEN: Most students of the novel would argue that novels need a lot of dreck. Dreiser can have an effect because all that unnecessary verbage has a cumulative power. Yours has a compressed impact line by line.

MORRIS: It isn't quite that bad, but it has something of that difficulty. Here I think is the crux of the matter. Never since 1951 or 1952 have I had to go back and reduce. What I begin to put down on the typewriter is already a précis. When I go through my early draft later, there isn't anything to take out. Usually I add things.

MADDEN: You say you weren't imitating Joyce with your epiphanies. You know that he went through a long period in which epiphanies were about all he wrote. When we look at the paragraphs in *In Our Time*, we see Hemingway doing a similar thing. Joyce and Hemingway represent the two stylistic poles that you work between. I don't see much stylistic similarity to Sherwood Anderson, despite your dedicating *The Works of*

Love to him. Only now and then does your tone sound like some of his sentences in *Winesburg, Ohio*. But I've noticed sometimes slight echoes of Gertrude Stein. Aside from *The Making of Americans,* what else interested you?

MORRIS: I like *Three Lives* very much. She had this great original gift for the music of the vernacular which seems to have no prehistory for her. Things she wrote before *Three Lives* were absolutely commonplace and pedestrian; she flowers without budding—everything in full bloom. As I was maturing I read no sophisticated fiction, no contemporary fiction, except Scott Fitzgerald's novel *This Side of Paradise*. I had no taste, I had no awareness of style whatsoever, until after I had been writing for about seven or eight years. Then I began to read to see what the hell it was all about.

I began as a natural product of my time like the grass that grows where the water is. Through my experience I had picked up a kind of rough-and-ready vernacular. I *was* Huck Finn. I did not have to be influenced by Twain. I was Tom Sawyer before I was Huck Finn. Of course I'd read *Tom Sawyer*—any kid who isn't illiterate has read *Tom Sawyer*. But by the time I began to write these novels about my childhood, I am already a stylist: a bad one. They're strange documents. If my work should eventually be of interest, these early novels will be of interest. They're damned juvenile, but they are *writing*.

MADDEN: A lot of young writers, when they begin to write, write in a pseudo-Victorian style, the style that they hated most when they were forced to read classics. You have said you read mainly nineteenth-century fiction. Did you ever try to write the pseudo-literary novel?

MORRIS: No, I was spared that. I was too naive to mimic anything. In my first two years at Pomona I was en-

couraged when they gave me a prize for Improvement. I
had a certain facility, not felicity, and after a year of
reading Spengler—four or five times—I wrote a kind of
fantasy in a heavy, solemn manner. I still have the
one-volume edition of *The Decline of the West*. One day it
will be a curio of interest. There's not a line in that book
that is not underlined once, twice, or three times. That is
the kind of reading that caught my fancy. I was fascinated by speculative ideas.

MADDEN: I have come to talking about your work as
the "novel of meditation." Does that ring true?

MORRIS: I think that is very viable. I pay necessary
attention to certain structural facts about the novel, and
I work on the pacing of a story in order to keep you
reading, to hold you against your will; but I never talk
about that because that I take for granted—if you know
how to walk, you don't spend the morning talking about
walking.

Essentially I'm concerned with consciousness. I need to
experience the full range of elements that appear in
what I am writing. If I were only telling a story, I
wouldn't bother to continue writing. Fiction is more than
action. I want to be able to meditate from page to page on
what the page is about.

MADDEN: Through your style and your techniques, you
have combined in one genre the essence of informal,
philosophical writing like Kierkegaard's, the essence of
the personal essay, the essence of poetry, and the essence
of fiction. This leads me to ask, did you ever write poems?

MORRIS: There is no need for me to write poems. I'm
writing poetry all the time.

MADDEN: Are *Bill of Rights* and all these other nonfiction books of a piece with the fiction? You really didn't

need to do them because philosophy and criticism and fiction are all of the same concern to you?

MORRIS: That is one of the shortcomings of *Bill of Rights*. I think it's an intelligent book, full of a great deal of fury. It's a book that's edgy all the way through. But it's not a book that's quite right. It's strained. Halfway through I said, What am I doing? Really, if there was anybody out there to speak to, they'd know. All of this is available in my fiction.

David, you have said that my style derived from a nonfiction kind of writing, and to me that requires some explanation.

MADDEN: I pointed out things like the parenthetical expression, your frequent use of "that is," and the word "as": "He shut the door *as* he was tired of listening to the wind." (I'm just making up the example.) These formal conjunctions, parenthetical expressions and the like are devices of style that I have always associated with formal writing. You usually use them in a mock formal way actually, but they do not seem to me to be fictive writing.

MORRIS: These details that you cite derive from my need to suggest a tone that is more detached, more in the manner of reporting, a tone not associated with an authorial eye or the eye of any one of the characters in the fiction. What you identify as "formal elements" provides a kind of passing scan of a scene. Your comment is so general that it might mislead somebody who was not familiar with my fiction.

MADDEN: I have also spoken of the "personal essay" which has a relatively formal tone compared to the informal tone of fiction. You use those formal phrases, even "however" sometimes, which seem to me to be very calculating, very self-conscious. You seem to want the detachment that simple, formalistic phrases will lend to a passage. Your novels are meditations; and in meditating, you are inclined to use formalistic kinds of constructions and syntax.

MORRIS: All of that is pertinent enough, but this formality is as much a fictive style as it is a nonfictive style. It is simply nonspecific, nonvernacular. My concern is to be able to use the vernacular without its extraordinary drawbacks and cul-de-sacs. It would be more accurate, it seems to me, to speak of my style as a fictive style modified to meet current and contemporary circumstances rather than a nonfiction style brought over into fiction. It is a fiction style which opens up, reappraises, the familiar clichéd vernacular.

MADDEN: My emphasis may be backwards. This is a fictive style into which are introduced certain nonfictive elements that modify it to lend a tone of distance, of authorial omniscience. From moment to moment, we have a kind of rhythm, from an emphasis on the vernacular to an emphasis on the formal. It comes down to the diction—"like," "as," "that is," "however," "would prove to be. . . ." Some people have said that Morris's style becomes sententious. They misread your use of these phrases.

MORRIS: They are suffering from what I'm attempting to cure them of. They are suffering from vernacularitis. They feel that if it's going to be fiction, it has to get down on its knees in a room where most people are standing or seated.

MADDEN: They assume that the diction has to be photographically and consistently true to the language of their experience. In one section of *About Fiction* you talk about how many writers (including David Madden in *The Brothers in Confidence*) rely so heavily on the sound of the narrating first-person voice—the way people really talk—that they don't get all the effects that are in their material. You want them to vary this first-person voice.

MORRIS: This limiting consistency is what I'm inveighing against, for a lot of reasons. Mine is a modified vernacular style to permit the intrusion of tones, moods, and qualities that ordinarily would be excluded from the vernacular. The variation in tone occurs in a writer working sixty-five years ago—Thomas Mann, a writer I admire and revere. It used to interest me how he would deliberately intrude Thomas Mann into his text; I admired the skill with which he did it. The intrusion was obvious to the writer who examined what he was doing, but nevertheless it was absolutely acceptable to the reader, because it was done with taste, with tact. By this intrusion Mann could give an added dimension to his characterizations. Without it, even though the characters were very cultivated, they could not reflect the depth of Mann's own imagination.

MADDEN: I noticed that in *Mario and the Magician.* Were you talking about this in English or in the original German?

MORRIS: I don't read German.

MADDEN: You mean in English you see this?

MORRIS: Heavens, yes. One of the interesting things about Mann's style is that it translates so well—in what is essential. In *Tonio Kröger*, in *Death in Venice,* Mann is intrusive time after time. It's very deliberate. You have the voice of Aschenbach, you have the voice of Tonio, and then there'll be a passage which is absolutely authorial. It does not come from anybody within the story, it comes from the outside, and Mann really does not feel the necessity that Joyce would have felt to be so subtle that you do not sense this intrusion.

MADDEN: You never intrude yourself as much as Mann does.

MORRIS: I labor to achieve the Mann aside without the Mann intrusion, to do it exactly as if I'm not there, but nonetheless to be there. In the vernacular style, customarily the tone has to be true to the character. I want the tone to be true to something that is larger than any individual character, to be part of the piece as a whole.

Take the tone at the start of *The Works of Love*. That just grows out of the sentiment, out of the mood of the moment. I had no technical approach to that material. I did not think, What would be a simple approach? I found my way into that story largely through tone, and I allowed tone to determine what was permissible and what was not permissible. I managed to work my way into a labyrinth from which eventually I had to withdraw by pulling back and shortening. It is of interest to me that I sensed the need for that tone not to be identified at the beginning. My natural inclination was for it to be the voice of a character we later meet.

MADDEN: Your authorial omniscient voice is employed in *The Works of Love* in a way that's different from your other books, except for isolated moments. You start and sustain a tone of relative objectivity, an author's tone, and the result, paradoxically, is that I feel more intimacy with Will Brady than I do with any of the characters whom you deliberately try to get inside of.

MORRIS: I think this is true. In a way the vernacular is concerned with putting forward the maximum information, tone, and movement of the story. Each voice must at times just talk and that voice may not be as revelatory as the author's can be. Each character is usually busy with his own little hang-ups.

MADDEN: And the vernacular is busy with another, usually transitory, experience. You experience vernacular intensely, but when it is over, it is really over. What saves your first-person vernacular stories, like *Love Among the Cannibals,* are those passages in which the narrator talks like an omniscient author, viewing the scene panoramically. If we didn't have those interludes in which the speaker philosophizes and mediates, the story would be like an oil slick—very quick. And relatively speaking, that is the effect of that novel: it shoots through your mind and right out again.

MORRIS: It is intended to create that illusion—and then later you find that your fingers are gummy. It's got to catch you and carry you and you say, "That was a fast read!" And then you suddenly find that the "fast read" has left bits of lint on your mind.

But there were many things going on in that book. Some I find successful, others I'm less satisfied with, but in the main it was the book that needed to be there. The book was a break; it ended my obsession with the reconstruction of the immediate past, and it moved me into the contemporary scene. I was very deliberate in that: the past had no existence in *Love Among the Cannibals.* It is the present as total. I was asking myself, Is it possible for me to invent a present that has no past?

MADDEN: This book put you in the tradition of the hard-boiled novel. These hard-boiled novels are totally obsessed with the present, in which the characters have absolutely no past. I compare it with James M. Cain. In his books all of the characters live absolutely in the immediate present.

MORRIS: I think the reader of my book experiencing the present will be involved in a needed reassessment of the past.

MADDEN: Yes, you are talking about the relation of the past to the present even though you didn't give us the narrator's past.

MORRIS: The stripping of the car is meant to be the metaphor for this situation. It should have all the overlays that any reader will bring to this particular experience.

MADDEN: It is the past that's being stripped symbolically by this action. The car is a past which has lasted only a few days. Of course the narrator has stripped himself of everything in his past, whatever that was; but also he is stripped of the immediate past, what he's had since he laid eyes on this girl only a few days before. During that time he was encumbered by all kinds of clichés.

MORRIS: That is right. And the past can be six hours. For a contemporary, the morning is the past. By noon it might have been the only past that has any consequence to him. The book was to suggest that the narrator's past had been encapsulated in his first experience with the girl. For the moment he is captured by a present in which the past is manufactured.

We speak constantly—we don't know how to do it otherwise—of the past, the present, the future. But in actual practice the present is that specific moment when the future is made into the past. What I said a moment ago is now past. We do what we can with our relatively limited faculties to develop a fiction to deal with time, with duration. We train ourselves to be metaphysically subtle and deliberately blind to how foolish we actually are. That's one of the tiresome things about metaphysics —there is more concealment in it than revelation.

MADDEN: But for all your impatience with talk of metaphysics and the like, you are constantly concerned with the mystical. Throughout your works you're always talking about the delayed effect that people who have died, or left, or are missing, have upon people who survive. That's essentially a humanistic kind of mysticism.

MORRIS: This awareness that you are never so alive (among the living) as when you are dead is one of the interesting psychological facts that relate cultures that appear to be different to one another—and relate various aspects of a single culture. When I began to reread Joyce's "The Dead," to see how he achieved—and more successfully than I did—this concept that the dead are always with us, frequently overshadowing the living, I realized that the dead on one level or another constitute our present, whether we will it or not. In certain cultural sensibilities, the dominance of the dead is what constitutes the culture, even to the point of stagnation. Joyce was convinced that the awareness of the presence of the dead with the living is really what makes up civilized behavior and civilized responses. The "presence" of those who are missing, who are physically absent, is the one immortality we can attest to.

MADDEN: You bring this up in your last two books, especially *A Life*. Yes, in *A Life* a man is getting in touch with his own death just a few hours before he experiences it. He is moving into death, and he becomes most alive; his perceptions, his sense of himself, are most intense just before he reaches that point of death.

MORRIS: If I were encouraged, or rather indulged, to speak in a fatherly fashion about *A Life*, I would say that it is something new in our literature. I have admitted to a native state of soul which is capable of a sort of transcendence, without benefit of the usual apparatus. Death is seen as neither an end nor a beginning, but a continuing process of nature to which the soul can be responsive. Sounds very mystical, doesn't it? I accept it as a fact in Warner's experience. He is not an intellectual, he is free of clichés and theories about death and dying, and on this day he senses that he will die, but finds he is remarkably tolerant toward it. He is neither stoically brave, nor spiritually panicked. He does not grasp why, but his nature accepts it: he gives himself to it. This is considered a transcendent experience for "higher forms" of life, but it is commonplace among most of God's creatures who have not cut their ties with nature. Curious how we assume that such a "natural" experience is mystical.

MADDEN: He neither escapes from life into death nor runs from death because he fears it. Suddenly he is close to it. He begins in wonder; to use your word, he looks at it in wonder. He doesn't feel abandoned, even by the loss of the boy; in fact, he abandons the boy himself.

MORRIS: It is all part of his stripping down to this ultimate experience. What is mystifying to me is how my imagination brought up that Indian. I had to have some figure free of the old man himself, free of the clichés associated with his situation, one who was almost an outsider and so could function as a kind of messenger. He comes with something that nobody understands. It attracts the old man, but he is also vaguely apprehensive. I did not calculate it; but I see that Blackbird is nature—and the nature that he represents is death. The old man senses this danger—but there is something in it he welcomes. He doesn't resist it; the Indian comes as a welcome executioner.

MADDEN: The Indian does not kill Warner as an act of vengeance against the white man, even though he has ideas of vengeance against the white man—or, rather, he has hatreds and resentments. In the drama of their relationship, he does not attach them to the old man.

MORRIS: His anger is too deep to be localized on one person, just as the old man's ignorance is too deep to be concerned with one Indian. They meet like two univer-salities who are combining for a moment, for a single, relatively inconsequential human event. But this event is all there is.

MADDEN: It's almost as if two alien stereotypes have come together and, having total incomprehension, relate to each other in all innocence. What happened is not growing out of character and past events. It operates on a totally mystical plane.

MORRIS: This situation can be formulated, can be thought up as a good idea for a story; but how it came about interests me almost as much as what came about. I felt absolutely assured in what I was doing, however strange it was. I was completely at ease with the unusual experience this old man was having. I felt its inevitabil-ity. There were just one or two moments when things had to happen in the story with that clicking rightness of a well-oiled mechanism. Through luck and circumstance, they did happen.

MADDEN: The act of experiencing this conception and the act of creating it were almost simultaneous? You didn't plan, plot, prefabricate?

MORRIS: Actually there's very little formulation in my fiction. As I write I'm usually only a few paragraphs ahead of myself. After maybe sixty or seventy-five pages I have a precognition of where I'd like to go, and so I begin to modifiably direct things, but never to the extent that I determine that a series of events will take place. I wait to see what these events are going to be. I talked to Wayne Booth about all this at some length.

MADDEN: When you wrote *Fire Sermon* did you know or expect or feel in your bones that there would be *A Life* coming up?

MORRIS: No. After I finished it, then I knew there would be something. I never had an idea that it would be what we have.

MADDEN: It could look as if you had written a whole thing which was the two novels and then said to yourself, Well, I think it would be more effective to publish half of it here and half of it there. Can you see how one might wonder if it came about in that fashion?

MORRIS: No, I don't really. I'm not able to read the books to get such an impression. You can. The reader can see relationships here that I would have to reread the books to acquire.

MADDEN: You mean a reader can know things about your books that you don't?

MORRIS: Certainly. You should have your own feelings, not necessarily a similar feeling to mine. I find it very tiresome for fiction to dictate the responses it evokes, as if the writer were manipulating his reader, saying, If you have these responses you are a good reader, if not, not. To the contrary. If I thought that I must produce predictable responses, I'd forget the whole thing. You should be free to have feelings of what is going to happen and react in your own way to what has happened. There are a variety of possibilities in every story. I provide the story, you provide the reaction. We all know things that we don't know we know. Many people have moments of relatively nonself inhibition and nonself awareness in which they reveal themselves to be superior to the selves that they "believe" themselves to be.

MADDEN: And you want your readers to collect imaginative responses that they may not even know they have?

MORRIS: The meaning of a scene is in the scene. When I attempt to get outside, to make sensible or even sympathetic comments about what is going on in a successful piece of fiction, like the death of Warner in *A Life,* I'm like any reader who attempts to explain what occurs within himself. A successful passage in fiction for a brief moment completes circuits that are usually broken, connects nerves and tissues we didn't know were there. We have the use, briefly, of sensations that are new, the tingling of life in a limb numb with sleep.

This is the experience Gabriel has in those last moments with Greta in Joyce's "The Dead." He goes through several extremes of life-enhancing self-awareness. Something of his old self-love has died, to be replaced by a new tenderness toward Greta, a healing sense of shame and pity toward himself. Over them both falls the snow that falls all over Ireland, and the commingled world of the living and the dead.

The Photography of Wright Morris
A Portfolio

PETER C. BUNNELL

Photographs hold a curious fascination for us that is not unlike the fascination of concise, descriptive prose. Although some photographs reflect their creator's aspiration to poetry, by and large it is the actuality of things as they are that is remarkably reflected in photographs. In a sense, photographs are highly literary; and the photographer, like the writer, has to be both a master of craft and a visionary. Patient accumulation of facts and then speculation about their meaning is the nature of authorship in both mediums. The speculation is often fictive—it may be untruthful. Perhaps untruthful is not quite the exact word. It might rather be said that the specificity of facts can give rise to heightened awareness which can evolve into heightened imagination. When considering the artist Wright Morris, we have in a single figure an exponent of the unity of word and picture. He seemingly found photography ready-made for his vision; and, importantly, he turned to it at a point in photography's evolution which found it ready-made to influence his vision.

Morris's most active photographic period spanned the decade ending in 1948. His work began out of his desire to master one kind of descriptive analysis—he wanted to treat objectifiable data so that man's artifacts could be presented as clues to the nature of existence. While it is generally assumed that the photographer is confined to reporting, Morris explores under the surface to reveal the significance beneath outer appearances. In his pictures Morris is interested in man's work—he has never been very much interested in nature. Not an anthropologist or a cultural historian, he is an exegete of action and values. Photography provided him with an objective sustained reality which enabled him to pose and solve problems of literal description. From this, as Morris has put it, the notion evolved, "that an accurate rendering of what was 'real' fulfilled the possibilities of fiction." He saw photography, in other words, as a synthesis—a drama combining the apparent duality of fact and fiction.

As a photographer Morris was more akin to the documentarians of photography's earliest period than to the contemporaneous social propagandists of America in the 1930s. Throughout much of the nineteenth century, photography was viewed as a kind of "self-operation" art in which the photographed object and the object itself were identical. Most photographers still act as though their pictures make factual statements: "This is a wall"; "This is a stove"; "This is a chair." Once one has recognized that photographs have their own meaning, however, they become open to several not mutually exclusive interpretations.

Morris reveals his approach to photography, and indeed to fiction, in the recent novel *Fire Sermon* (1971). In it he focuses on a young boy, who, after observing the household of a relative, is eloquently described by Morris, "He brought so little to what he saw, he saw what was there." This is an identification of what exists with what is seen and is characteristic of the demanding approach of the documentary. It requires a balance between the contextual environment of the photograph and the photographed image so that the picture projects its content directly and can be read simply, even by the inexperienced. Morris aligns himself with a few photographers of his generation: Walker Evans, Russell Lee, and perhaps to a lesser extent Paul Strand. A similar approach can be seen in the earlier work of Atget and, more recently, in Diane Arbus and Robert Adams. These photographers do not abandon or deny artifice, but they aspire to suggest absolutes beyond it.

Early in his work, Morris was not far removed from certain straightforward pictorial documentarians, like Minor White, who with Morris and others were shown in a revealing thematic exhibition at The Museum of Modern Art in 1941 entitled, "The Image of Freedom." These photographers of the late 1930s rejected both the social realism of the Farm Security Administration school and the Stieglitz—Weston aesthetic. They had moved toward a pictorialism devoid of the tricks or charms often associated with the 1920s formalist style and concentrated more explicitly on human values. After about 1941 Morris turned to photographic problems even further removed from pictorialism; that is, he found his true métier in the specificity of things themselves. His photographs of this later period were taken at close range, unemotionally; they were almost gritty in their texture, insistently factual, and they reflected Morris's increasing concern with the vernacular artifact.

A photographer can minimize the pictorial by stressing the subject of his picture, its factual presence, and its identity with a social environment. The finest documentary photography offers us a picture which is organically unified around a subject. This controlled unity is the key to Morris's work. His images are not tempered with sentimentality but restrict themselves to recording the qualities of the subjects. By examining Walker Evans, who had published *American Photographs* (1938) during the time Morris was working, one can compare varying states of passivity and activism. In their quest for realism, both men take a static, frontal approach to their subjects; but the self-conscious frontality and framing of a Morris image exploits the fragmenting properties of photography. By calling attention not only to the arbitrariness of angle but to the edge of the picture, Morris refers to the world outside the limits of the picture. One is made forcefully aware that the rooms of the Home Place extend beyond what is pictorially presented, that a world exists beyond the world of the image. It is not the naturalism of the image that provokes this awareness but the degree of stylization in the picture. Morris does not glimpse reality, but he stares at it and, when at his best, lets it reveal itself.

Although Morris's photographs are part of his artistic development as well as part of the history of American photography, their intrinsic values remain. His two photograph-text novels, *The Inhabitants* (1946) and *The Home Place* (1948), are landmarks of their genre, brilliantly exploring a most complex form. In these books, pictures and fiction confront one another on opposite pages. They are described by some as "novels-cum-photographs"—most readers have found that the photographs "crush" the prose. But Morris never intended to harmonize the fiction and the pictures as Nancy Newhall and Paul Strand harmonized them in *Time in New England* (1950). Rather, he forged a kind of counterpoint out of the instrinsic characteristics of each medium in order to go for a larger statement. By juxtaposing picture and text, he set out to make each more, not less, than it was alone. He wanted to capitalize on the uniquenesses in each. A comparison may be made to the James Agee—Walker Evans volume, *Let Us Now Praise Famous Men* (1941). In combining pictures and text Agee and Evans used a classic, separatist format. The pictures here are separated into two "books"—all pictures together, then all text. In Morris's books, we do not read the photographs as illustrations nor the text as elaborated captioning. Morris uses words to describe the world that the photographs allude to, a world omitted in the pictures. The prose and the pictures are designed to function as a single unit.

Recently in *God's Country and My People* (1968) Morris has again used his photographs in conjunction with his prose. While highly autobiographical and refined in form, this book strives to provide examples of what might be salvaged for another generation. Morris exhibits his confidence in the timelessness of his approach to photography and to the photographic object. Nostalgia is not an issue. Instead, in this latest volume the photographs provide a checklist of the significant values which comprise the continuing American experience.

This portfolio of photographs includes works by Wright Morris as well as works by photographers whose pictures illuminate the qualities of Morris's pictures. Of particular import is the comparison of Morris to Walker Evans. Significant for both are such earlier precursors of the documentary style as the Frenchman, Eugène Atget, and the anonymous cameraman working for Mathew Brady. A contemporary exponent of the documentary approach may be seen in the work of Robert Adams, whose photograph is reproduced from his book *The New West* (1974).

All of the photographs have been selected to illustrate observations made in my text and in the conversation between Wright Morris and myself. The images manifest a view of the documentary as a genre and should be read as a statement parallel to my text. Through the layout the photographs are presented as works in themselves, with individual integrity.

I. Wright Morris: Farm House with White Chimney from Cornfield, near Culpeper, Virginia, 1940

II. Wright Morris: Model T Ford with California Top, Ed's Place, near Norfolk, Nebraska, 1947

III. Wright Morris: View into Kitchen, Ed's Place, near Norfolk, Nebraska, 1947

IV. Walker Evans: Farmer's Kitchen, Hale County, Alabama, 1936
Courtesy of the Library of Congress, Washington

V. Anonymous Cameraman for Mathew Brady: Castle Pinckney, Charlestown, South Carolina, c. 1863
Courtesy of the Library of Congress, Washington

VI. Eugène Atget: A la Biche, Rue Geoffroy St. Hilaire, Paris, 1922
Collection of Peter C. Bunnell

VII. Robert Adams: Frame for a Tract House, Colorado Springs, Colorado, 1968
Courtesy of the photographer

VIII. Wright Morris: Outhouse and Backstop, Nebraska, 1947

IX. Wright Morris: Straight-backed Chair by Door, The Home Place, near Norfolk, Nebraska, 1947

X. Wright Morris: Dresser Drawer, Ed's Place, near Norfolk, Nebraska, 1947

XI. Wright Morris: Wellfleet, White House, Cape Cod, Massachusetts, 1939

XII. Wright Morris: Meeting House, Southbury, Connecticut, 1940

Wright Morris's photographs are reproduced courtesy of the photographer

I

II

III

IV

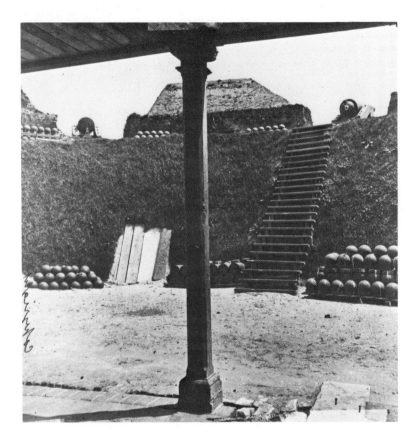

V

VI

VII

VIII

IX

X

XI

XII

Photography and Reality

A Conversation between
Peter C. Bunnell and Wright Morris

Morris: Peter, let's work around your idea of the photograph as a mirror and some of the modifications you made in playing with it. The mirror is one of the durable and inexhaustible metaphors we use in the interpretation of what we think constitutes reality.

Bunnell: The nineteenth-century way of looking at the photograph was as a mirror for the memory, and at that time the photographs almost looked like a mirror, with their polished and metallic surfaces. But really the photograph presents a kind of reality that isn't a mirror. It reflects yourself. You see in the photograph what you are. You recognize content only as you have ability to identify and then to interpret.

Morris: To what extent do you feel that might have been a reasonably common impression in the nineteenth century? Weren't most people overwhelmed just by the seeing of the self? Didn't they see the standard daguerreotype image as an object reflecting reality?

Bunnell: Yes, they saw it as presenting the facts. Talbot's book, published in 1844, was the first to be illustrated entirely with photographs and it was called *The Pencil of Nature.* The image seemed to engrave itself without intervention. In effect, I think they didn't interpret at all. I think they saw in the photograph what they would look at in some of yours: the artifact, the thing itself. Only later after the daguerreotype process was superseded by more manipulative processes and the potentiality of altering the picture was known did the idea of the photograph as a new object really come into general understanding.

MORRIS: Was there anyone preceding Atget who seemed to be aware of the possibilities of transposing what is commonly accepted as the actual over into a possessed object separate from a mirror reflection? What about the French photographer, Niépce?

BUNNELL: There were hundreds of photographers who saw, as you did, possibilities of transposing reality, but most of them are anonymous today. I think we must look for schools or bodies of photographic works rather than individuals. I've always felt, for instance, that in American daguerreotypes—specifically in the portraits but in photographs of objects as well—the clarity and precision indicate that the photographers sensed a joining of process and object. There is always this sense of moving toward a more pictorial sensibility, where the photographic object supersedes in effect the fundamental integrity of the subject photographed.

MORRIS: The inclination is always to supersede.

BUNNELL: A lot of daguerreotypists didn't know that they were doing this. Their early manuals are fascinating because they told you everything. They are cookbooks. They told you how to get to the point of making one of those pictures but never what to make. In a way, they really had no other option than to respect the integrity of what they took the picture of. It really was only later that they began to see for itself what they had made.

When did you first know of Atget, Wright?

MORRIS: I think I saw my first Atget photographs in 1939 or 1940. An art editor from the *New York Times* gave me a group of them. I had had this little show at the New School for Social Research which he had seen, and he asked if I would be interested. There were hardly any prints of those photographs available at that time, and I had no sophistication whatsoever. But I did know of Atget, and yes, I wanted the photographs. It happened to be a marvelous group, just a marvelous group. It absolutely startled me that anybody should be seeing in such a manner at that time. That sense of being plagiarized before you are born is very tiresome!

BUNNELL: But were you conscious after that time that Atget influenced what you were seeing and doing?

MORRIS: He gave me reassurance and a sense of persistence. Now I think maybe five of those first pictures may have been portraits of women, his whore series, you know, which were extraordinary because they were so absolutely, beautifully detached and yet so good. The person is there, the situation is there, and they provided an effect of extraordinary bleakness by their sepia tone in contrast to the Paris atmosphere: it's bloodchilling. And then there were a couple taken out in the woods. There was one of a tree. I also had a picture of a tree and roots; and I felt, given the same circumstances, Atget's was a picture I would have taken. That simultaneous existence at different times of the same sensibility has always fascinated me. What I later came to was a kind of metaphysical conviction that we really don't possess anything—we are merely the inheritors of a sensibility that moves among us. This awareness of a common sensibility gives the reassurance that I think we seek in immortality.

BUNNELL: The photograph has a strong sense of that, of immortality. In the introduction to your Venice book, *Love Affair: A Venetian Journal* [1972], you talk about salvaging the experiences of the city. This suggests the transitory nature of the thing itself and that the photograph serves to salvage, to monumentalize, to make permanent.

MORRIS: The word *salvage* is quite misleading and needs to be taken out and honed and broken down and reconsidered. Like any writer, I fall into a period when a word seems fresh and I grab onto it and it's gratifying, and then I wear the word out, and I come back to it, and I say, This word is bearing the burden of half a dozen other words and I don't like it so much any more. I'm beginning to have that feeling about *salvage*. I am just about prepared to turn it in for a retread. I am about to fall under the persuasion of my own rhetoric, so to speak; but it has an origin in an impulse that is authentic.

As an American of a certain period, I have built into me a certain sensitivity to "the arrears of our culture." I have an instinctive rejection of the fact that we constantly replace. We can speak of this habit as destroying or we can speak of it as progressive replacement, but I don't like it. There is operative in me an effort to put back the sand pile after the water has come in and washed it away. But that tendency does not serve as a real point of motivation. It is merely one of a variety of responses. When I use the word *salvage* in too general a way, I allow myself to oversimplify and turn what is a very complex relationship with an artifact into something that is quite misleading. If somebody says: Really, man, you're just trying to hang onto things that naturally have to be replaced; a kind of nostalgic mania and, basically, although this has a certain attraction and will keep you preoccupied when you're not suffering from migraine, it really leads nowhere; and furthermore it does not constitute what your photographs really seem to be concerned with—I would have to say, Correct. Nostalgia is merely one ingredient.

Only at a certain point am I concerned with a holding action. You remember the Beckett quotation in the front of *God's Country and My People:* "From things about to disappear I turn away in time. To watch them out of sight, no, I can't do it." That speaks deeply to me. Very deeply. We're dealing here with the *zeitgeist.* Perhaps everyone in this century is insecure about the persistence of the past. But there is something different too. In all artists there is something operating deliberately which is ordinarily concealed. I think there is present in any construction an effort to replace what is disappearing. I think it is like the replanting of crops.

BUNNELL: Is the photograph the replacement?

MORRIS: No, I'm thinking simply of any act that is imaginative or creative. That act appears simply to emerge, out of our nature. I talked about this to Wayne Booth the other day (see pages 89 ff.). I am myself convinced that the imaginative activity is organic and that the mind thinks just as a plant gives off buds, and that the depression of the faculty inhibits man and destroys something basic in him. It is an absolute necessity for the mind, like the hands, to replace what is wearing out, to replace the cost of living. We can think and talk about art, talk about all its infinite labyrinthine experimentation, and forget that it comes out of this need to hold on to what is passing. The artist says, "Don't give up! Keep ahold!" Now the photograph cuts through the aesthetic of some of the more inwardly turned and inwardly developed crafts—like, let us say, contemporary painting. Just as writing resists some of the worst forms of erosion, I think photography resists them too. With both photography and writing, beyond a certain point what you do just isn't comprehensible, and you have to come back to the point of departure.

BUNNELL: You mean that the photo and writings are alike in that both are things in themselves and also refer to a reality aside from themselves?

MORRIS: These two sides of photography are something of a mania with me, and I've repeatedly talked about it. There's even a passage in *Love Affair*, if you remember, about giving up one picture to get another. That was as tactful a way as I could find to say that the camera is the first obstruction between us and experience. I think this is both subtle and almost inevitable. When you begin to be lens-oriented, the object itself is secondary and you wait to see later what it is you've done. On repeated occasions I have been very vague about what I have done, knowing that I'd see later, or I wouldn't see at all, why I had taken the picture. I waited. I *had* had a shock of recognition, but what it was, I would learn later. And sometimes I have learned from the photograph— that is, in the photograph I frequently learn the possibilities of the photograph. This is what happened, precisely, with the intrusion of my shadow in the picture of the Model T Ford. [Plate II shows the right side of the car drawn up in the farmyard.] In the foreground you can see the shadow of the photographer and his camera between the edge of the picture and the car itself. At first I wanted to eliminate that shadow. It was a distraction toward which I had no ambivalence at all. I just wanted to get it out of there, and unable to get it out satisfactorily, I put the picture aside as one that I was not going to try to get into the book I was writing. It became a kind of secondary picture. Then coming back, about three years later, I saw that picture for the first time, and I said, Well! and I looked at it and I attempted to make an adjustment to the variety of impressions I was having from it. Gradually it began to win me over.

BUNNELL: In Plate I is exactly the same kind of intrusion. The photographer's hand and his box get between us and the haystack and house which are the subject of the picture. That was made in 1940.

MORRIS: I'm in sympathy with what I learn from the scene itself, and I do not reject what I found in that picture, saying, My God, there's another intrusion! We'll just cut it off up here.

Under different circumstances something like this could have led me into a very different area of photographic experiment. But obsessed as I was with my material, I thought of it only as an incident. The possibilities and the limitations of photography can be almost summed up in this type of encountered reflection. If you are a photographer, you are obsessed with some concept of actuality. You do not want to diminish the essence of your statement, and then gradually it comes upon you that you are working as a picture maker. And so you have to reconsider and become a little less inflexible about what the medium really should be doing. At first you think you have rather clear ideas about this; it is the so-called straight photography approach. Getting away from that would have taken me considerable time, although it was inevitable—if I hadn't been diverted by the demands of writing. I did not at that point have to make the next step photographically because I was completely preoccupied as a writer.

BUNNELL: Does anything analogous occur in the writing? Do you face that shadow image when you are writing fiction?

MORRIS: Yes, the problems of the craft of fiction are not necessarily concerned with the intrusion of the writer, but they are similar in that the writer must move from one level of dealing with his experience to another level. I've never had to deal with the craft of photography as with writing, however, because by the time I reached the end of that first photographic statement, I was faced with a do-or-die challenge to simplify and make my way as a writer independent of my photography.

BUNNELL: You began your career in the thirties, and anybody who had to live through the thirties unfortunately acquired a kind of social-realist tag. You got it, but I don't think it is applicable, even though you must have been aware of the realistic photographic activity of agencies like the Farm Security Administration. Did you meet Roy Stryker of the FSA and offer to go out on tour, taking pictures of the country as they hired photographers to do in those days?

MORRIS: I was prepared to lay my hands on money if I could. I went to see Stryker, though I had at that time begun to be reasonably suspicious of his eye. He looked through a portfolio I had brought in—flipped through the pages the way a man does who has looked at too many photographs—and commented that the sort of thing I was doing was not at all what they were doing in the Department. I said I knew that but I simply wanted to show him my stuff.

BUNNELL: Were you ever in fact primarily concerned with the social implications of your pictures?

MORRIS: I still have this problem. The similarity of my subjects—abandoned farms, discarded objects—to those that were taken during the depression, and were specifically taken to make a social comment, distracts many observers from the *concealed* life of these objects. This other nature is there, but the cliché of hard times, of social unrest, of depression, ruin, and alienation, is the image the observer first receives. Perhaps it can't be helped. All, or most, photographs have many faces. The face desired is revealed by the caption. I do not have captions, but the facing text reveals the nature of the object that interests me: the life of the inhabitants whose shells they are, as Thoreau said. The social comment may well be intense, but it is indirect, and not my central purpose. These objects, these artifacts, are saturated with emotion, with implications, toward which I am peculiarly responsive. I see many of them as secular icons. They have for me a holy meaning they seek to give out. Only a few, of course, speak out with this assurance, but if the observer is attentive he will be attuned to my pictures and how it is they differ from most others. Once that is clear, they do not need captions. He is open to the same responses I am.

Although that problem is always present, the phototext confronted me with many others. Chief among them is that some people are readers, some are lookers. The reader becomes a more and more refined reader, with less and less tolerance for distractions. In my own case, I cannot abide illustrations in a good novel. They interfere with my own impressions. The pictures I need are on my mind's eye. Now the relatively pure *looker* will subtly resent what he is urged to read. He wants all *that* in the picture. Each of these sophisticated specialists resents the parallel, competing attraction. As you have pointed out, Peter, the photograph requires a "reading," as well as a looking—its details scrutinized in a knowledgeable manner. In my case, this was a crisis. If the photograph overpowered the text, or if the reader treated the text lightly, I had defeated my original purpose. It was also crucial for my publisher, who considered me a novelist. *The Home Place* was well received, but pointed up this dilemma. I was losing readers, picking up lookers. Several reviewers asked why this ex-photographer was writing fiction. There was only one way to clear this up. Stop the photo-books. And so I did.

BUNNELL: What was your present publisher's motivation in coming back to the photo-text book?

MORRIS: Me, I was on the verge of changing publishers, along with my editor, and I used the occasion to slip in *God's Country and My People,* a reconsideration and reappraisal of my photographs.

BUNNELL: In *God's Country* you use the same photographs that are in *The Home Place* plus obviously more. This is a different, explicitly autobiographical kind of text. Could the photographer's shadows in some of the photographs be a kind of self-portrait presence like the autobiographical text of *God's Country*?

MORRIS: You are getting very close to why I felt it necessary to do that book, and why I did it in that manner. It's a reconsideration of material from a later point in time, using essentially the same techniques and the same body of photographs. It was the quality of the repetition that was necessary to this book. Both the writing and the photographs undergo a sea change in the overview taken by the writer. I didn't know what problems I would have with readers who understandably might take offense and say, What is he doing in repeating himself! But I couldn't go out and make a new world for myself to photograph, and it wasn't advisable. This is a revisitation. In fact, a repossession. But there weren't enough such readers to make any difference. Nobody raised this problem at all.

BUNNELL: Now that you are back in Nebraska, in a real revisitation, you must be challenged to deal again with things that you dealt with before, after, or through another point in time. One might ask, Why doesn't he try to find if the values which he tried to exemplify in the barber pole of 1940, say, are really of value now. What is Nebraska now? In other words, what does a writer and an artist who has this time span, do? It's something that a person my age can't answer.

MORRIS: I think this is not only a number one problem for me, I think it's also a number one problem for people of your generation. There is a diminishment of value in the artifact itself, and there is a limited way in which a photographer can deal with the diminished values of the contemporary artifact. There is a statement to be made about them, but it will be relatively shallow, soon exhausted. Young photographers, of course, orient themselves toward this problem much more positively, but I think aesthetically they face the same problem that I am aware of, the poverty of significance in the artifacts themselves. And when I come back into this old environment, I am startled by the relative richness of the old and the lack of it in the new. We call it progress. We make it new, but we do not love what we make.

BUNNELL: Judging from a photograph of your own house, you are not yourself much of a collector. I mean your house doesn't seem to be filled with artifacts, with objects. You don't seem to need things, however much you describe and photograph them.

MORRIS: What photograph did you see? Our house is bulging, but it's not a museum. Our friends get a contrary impression—or is it the difference between the actual room and a photograph of it?

BUNNELL: Here is a reinforcement of a kind of parallelism and divergence that I was setting up between yourself and Walker Evans. Evans collected like a maniac. When he photographed the neon pop sign in Alabama, he brought it back home with him. The photograph transformed it and he knew that he dominated it. Though he loved the subject, it wasn't of interest to him in his art. The picture was important, not the subject of the picture. So he brought the neon pop sign home. Look at a photograph of his place and of other photographers', and you find more than just lived-in clutter. They're surrounded by collectable artifacts, actual things. You are not.

MORRIS: I'd say it works in reverse with me. If I have the photograph, I can dispense with the artifact. The mobility of my life has made it impractical to hold onto more than books. But not showing in the photograph of our living room is an entrance and a hallway which has a group of my photographs. These constitute artifacts. In a sense they hang there by accident, not design. They were framed and put up for a Guggenheim exhibition; and when the show was over, they were sent back to me. Now it fascinates me that Evans would have had a need to latch onto actual artifacts. It's idle for me to speculate, but I wonder if there's a difference in our backgrounds. Was he mostly a city man?

BUNNELL: Yes.

MORRIS: I think that would make a big difference.

BUNNELL: I don't mean to say that what he collected was necessarily remnants of Alabama tenant farmers' houses. He was a great Victoriana collector—paperweights, and white marble rubbings—bric-à-brac I guess you'd call it. Coming back to Nebraska now, have you gone or have you any inclination to go back to these places that you lived in and photographed?

MORRIS: My God, yes. But our car was banged up soon after our arrival, during the period we had both the time and the weather. We did get over to Central City, my home place, with the local television people; incidentally, they are doing a piece called *Repossession*—we will see if it works. The Home Place, lock, stock, and barrel, was bulldozed out of existence in the late fifties. Nothing remains but what we have in the book, which does speak up for salvage. For a few days I did take a few pictures to see if there was a change in my way of looking at similar artifacts. But it was not noticeable. Much that speaks personally to me is still around, but I see little that is new that attracts me. I assume that younger photographers see it differently, but local work that I have seen is past-oriented, reflecting the vogue in nostalgia and "antiques." I sense there is a quandry in what they should "take." And if they take *that* today, what will they do tomorrow? The vast number of photographers, feeding on anything visible, overgraze the landscape the way cattle overgraze their pasture. As in the novel, there is overproduction and underconsumption. You would know about this, and I wouldn't. In the way of *artifacts,* which is close to my experience, what is it that the young photographer loves?—or that he hates to the point of revelation? Revealing what that *is* is the one thing that still doesn't come with the camera. Or will that be next?

Origins

Reflections on Emotion, Memory, and Imagination

WRIGHT MORRIS

In my second novel, *The Man Who Was There*, published in 1945, a character ponders the ceaseless accumulation of lint and dust under the bed. Where, she wonders, does it all come from? After almost forty years of fiction writing I am led to ask the same question. Is it substantially imagination, or memory? It is well known that fiction writers have long memories, and draw on them often. So do most people, or the writer's memory would be of little interest. In the main he reminds us of what we remember about ourselves. In much of modern fiction we seem to see more of memory than imagination. Writers remember what happened, then embellish on it, even if it happened only last week. I still have a vivid memory of the occasion my own memory was singled out for admiration. "What a memory you have!" the reader told me, who happened to be from my home state of Nebraska. He could testify that what I remembered was part of the truth, if not all of it. "I was right there," he said, "but I'd forgotten most of it. Reading your book brought it all back." I thanked him. It was not a small thing to bring it all back, whatever it was.

I have been more attentive to memory, since my debt was pointed out. Was that what I was doing? Remembering what others had forgotten? That reader had particular praise for what I remembered about Lone Tree, the site of *Ceremony in Lone Tree.* I had been too pleased (and tactful) to suggest that Lone Tree had no existence in fact but was the fabrication of a writer who showed little or no total recall. Lone Tree was to be found only in the novel, not on the map. Regrettably, this admission disenchants many readers and leads them to question the writer's sources. How is one to know he knows what he is doing? This reader particularly liked a chapter in the novel called *The Scene,* seeded with the objects and the details in which I seem to take so much interest. There was that fly at the window, the one trapped between the cracked blind and the pane. How well the reader remembered that identical fly! He also recalled how, as a boy, he had buried the white hairs pulled from a mare's tail in a barrel of rainwater, but it had skipped his mind what had then happened, if anything. For filling him in on all of that, he was grateful. This reader could appreciate, as many could not, who had not been born and raised in the Platte Valley, the pleasure of tagging along, barefoot, in the wake of the watersprinkler. He felt sure he had seen that particular sprinkler on his last trip back.

His comment reminded me that my own bare feet had gone unsprinkled. A real loss or a slip of memory? In another town, led on by a scoundrel, I repeatedly looted an ice wagon. In the ice we sucked, strange things were frozen. What they were I was free to imagine. Is it in such a manner that the fiction writer redeems lost time?

I see now that much of my plains-based fiction grew out of my need for an experience I came too late for. The signal example is the town of Lone Tree itself, first observed, in passing, in *The World in the Attic,* a suitable realm and dwelling place for the likes of Tom Scanlon. Once that fact was determined, the appropriate details assembled about his person. They settled into their places, their roles, as icons: a hotel, a lone tree, a railroad, a cattle loader. These artifacts constituted "the scene" in the way movable props located a Western movie.

Like Uncle Fremont, in *Cause for Wonder,* I came too late for God and too early for the Farm Security Administration. A boy of nine, I left the Platte Valley ignorant of the fact that my home town of Central City had once been called Lone Tree. Neither relate to Lone Tree, the home of Tom Scanlon, and the site of the ceremony in the novel. All of that town is a fiction, an assemblage of roles, parts and missing pieces, saturated with sentiment and reminiscence, brought in at night, under the cover of darkness, and discovered casting real shadows in the morning. Some of this fabrication derived from fiction (over the years I had seen photographs and read frontier journals) but all of it had been processed by the emotion rooted in my boyhood experience. The emotion was what mattered. It would do with the shards of memory all that it could.

When we say, "How well I remember!" we invariably remember rather poorly. It is the emotion that is strong, not the details. The elusive details are incidental, since the emotion is what matters. In this deficiency of memory, in my opinion, we have the origins of the imagination. To repossess we must imagine: our first memories are as dim as they are lasting. Until recorded history, memory constituted history and memory processed by emotion was our only means of repossession. When this is done with appropriate craft we define it as art. Minds differ in the extent they possess the faculty of memory, and how it is processed, but I note in my own certain characteristics that I believe are common to image-making. It is emotion that generates image-making: it is emotion that processes memory. That each artist will process it in his own manner is the hallmark of creative image-making, as distinct from the inventions of fancy. One of the handicaps of science fiction and fantasy is that the image-making is free of the emotion that is characteristic of processed memory, of repossessed life. The mind is often at play, like the summer night buzzing with insects, but to imagine, to make an image, to shape, assemble, and structure, differs from the play of fancy and idle dreaming through the energy it receives from emotion—the degree of this energy is immeasureably low in fiction for "light summer reading."

Image-making begins in earnest where memory fades. The skein of memory is often so frail we see right through it, and it frays at the edges. Invoking its presence is similar to a seance. Is it really *him,* we wonder, or an imposter? Imagination can be lured, but not willed, to do this restoration for us. In good fiction we can usually distinguish those portions that are craftily willed from those winged with imagination. Without the gossamer of memory it is less than life, with it as a ground it proves to be more. First we make these images to see clearly: then we see clearly only what we have made. Over forty years of writing what I have imagined has replaced and overlapped what I once remembered. The fictions have become the facts of my life.

One of our necessary illusions is that we see things as a "whole." If someone says "Look at the wall," and the wall is empty, what we see is blankness. If the wall is a mural, or hung with pictures, or covered with graffiti, the eye must focus on each object separately or see nothing distinctly. We get a "general impression," lacking in details, or we get details without the general impression. A trained eye hopes to get both, as when the critic studies a painting, or the artist studies a landscape, but what we see on the mind's eye of memory is seldom clearly one or the other. An overlapping of many "snapshots," in the manner of a cubistic painting, creates a vibrant or jumbled image that constitutes our impression. The mind is an archive of these sensations. In their infinite variety they surely exhibit individual and general characteristics. Nabokov says, "Speak memory!" but memory is not Hamlet's ghost. It is Nabokov who speaks. On this gauzelike tissue and from these competing fragments the writer chooses and assembles his own pictures. The reader says, "What a memory you have!" but it is what escapes the memory that stirs the imagination.

In the Moldavanka ghetto of Odessa, the child, Isaac Babel, liked to sit under a table, peering out at the world.

> As a boy I was given to lying. It was all due to reading. My imagination was always on fire. I read in class, during recess, on the way home, at night—under the dinner table, hidden by the folds of the cloth that reached down to the floor. Reading made me miss all the important doings of this world.[1]

In these few words light is shed on the subject of fiction and the imagination. Not all writers burn with this fire, but many had their beginnings *under* something. This might be crucial to the act of creation. Far from Odessa, in the Platte Valley of Nebraska, street culverts, piano boxes, storm caves, outhouses, and the dark caves under porches were favored places of concealment. I shared with other small creatures of this world Bre'r Rabbit's instinct to lie low. Seated in dust fine as talcum, my lap a pattern of leaf and slat shadows, I peered out at the world. A train passed, the street darkened with shadows, a tethered cow grazed, sparrows hopped from the wires to the ditch grass, the bell tinkled on the Jewel's Tea Wagon as it rocked on the tracks.

1. Isaac Babel, *Benya Krik, The Gangster and Other Stories* (New York: Schocken Books, 1969), p. 65.

If I see it all clearly, one reason might be that I have so often put it into writing, replacing a vague image with a sharp one. This in turn led to another impression, as I labored at the business of writing. Like the observer of flying objects, I was eager to make clear what seemed so elusive on the mind's eye.

Not long ago I returned to the town I was born in, to the house I associated with my childhood. The porch of this house proved to be a stoop, less than a foot off the ground. A cat might have crawled beneath it, but not a plump child. Other porches were available nearby, but not with the view I had described so clearly. Was I, then, so prematurely a fiction writer?

Referring both to what was written, and what I remembered, I noted other details. The porch was used to store a pair of stilts, a scooter made from a skate, and a Flexible Flyer sled on which I sometimes sat, fizzing soda pop. This Flexible Flyer came late in my boyhood, there being little excuse for it in the flat Platte Valley. Along with the scooter, it came with a porch that sat five steps higher than the sidewalk with adequate sitting room beneath it. Dividing the porch was a swing that creaked and scraped the paint off the house clapboards. A walk curved around the house to the yard at the rear, and seated beneath the porch I would watch the legs pass. A very suitable porch in every way, but in hilly Omaha, and not the Platte Valley.

In the fullness of time I substituted this porch, superior for purposes of observation, for the stoop attached to the house in the Platte Valley. The view was not much, obstructed as it was by the second-floor windows of the neighboring house. When not counting marbles or eating tootsie rolls, I brooded on the life behind the curtained windows. A giant of a man, Mr. Sluzak, lived there with his child-size wife. He drove a big truck for the Railway Express and wore overalls with shoulder straps, like a farmer. His daughter, Lillian, showed the tops of her stockings when we played Run Sheep Run under the street light.

If I attempt to distinguish between fiction and memory, and press my nose to memory's glass to see it more clearly, the remembered image grows more immaterial, flickering and insubstantial as reflections on water, or the details of a pointillist painting. The very vividness of the memory is matched by the vagueness of the impression. My recognition is a vibrant fabric of emotion, rippling like silk on which scenes have been painted. These wavering, insubstantial images haunt the memory, they taunt and lure the imagination. If I remembered both vividly and accurately the image-making faculty would be blocked, lacking the need to affirm what is vague or fill in what appears to be empty. Precisely where memory is frail and imperfect, imagination takes fire.

In the clutter of what is remembered and what is imagined some things prove to be symbolic objects. They gather lint. They were in rather than out.

> A bent skate key
> A needle with a burned point
> A ball of tinfoil
> A street car token (found among coins in a
>   city without street cars)
> A gumball machine
> The cracked chimney of a lamp

Artifacts mystically quickened with sentiment and emotion await their reappearance in the imagination, a reenactment and a confirmation. Each time these tokens are handled they give off light.

A few lines back, I was distracted by images embalmed in a fluid of emotion. They came involuntary at the thought, the *image* of, a porch. I had neither seen nor been on it or beneath it for more than fifty years. Now I noted where the chain swing whacked the clapboards, scraping off the paint. I remarked how the breeze stirred the curtains at the window: that the smell of a warming icebox oozed out of the hallways. Behind the screen door a gas jet burned, hissing in its mantle, like a finger held to the lips. Quiet was invoked. The master of the house, who worked nights and slept days, was trying to sleep.

> On the dresser in the bedroom, where it ticked loudly, he would put out his railroad watch, on its chain, with the small gold knife that he used to clean the grease from his nails. Until he shaved at the kitchen window where just his lathered head showed above the curtain, he wore his snug whipcord pants with the straps of his braces dangling, his underwear unbuttoned to expose the crinkly hair on his chest. Nothing could have been more commonplace, but it left on Cowie a lasting impression. No ordinary mortal arose so late in the day and walked around as he did, wearing harness, as if unhitched from the work he had accomplished while asleep. [*One Day,* pp. 76–77]

I was reluctant to surrender myself to this scene, feeling that I was spying on my own imagination. Unmentioned, but sharp to my senses, is the surrounding presence of a summer morning and the scorched smell of the iron on the draft from the kitchen. In all of this a memory fragment has been processed by emotion—the scorched smell of ironing, the tick of a watch, a lathered face above a half-curtained window—emerging as a new, more gratifying image. An assembly of separate, dispersed impressions, is filtered through a persistent and cherished emotion. The swing creaks, the blind sucks in at the window, water drips in the pan under the icebox.

The American writer, for self-evident reasons, often beginning with the disorder of creation, is "subject to the superstition that objects and places, coherently grouped, disposed for human use and addressed to it, must have a sense of their own, a mystic meaning to give out."

This testimony links Henry James to the object-and-place obsessed imaginations of Whitman and Twain. Image-making exorcises this obsession. A sled by the name of Rosebud, or a similar object, around which sentiment and emotions cluster, waits on the moment that a larger image will provide for its salvage, and release from darkness. How appropriate it is that the fledgling artist tests his faculties on these first impressions. Soon enough he will see more than he remembers, and observe more than he imagines, but the clue to his image-making will be found among the potsherds of his first impressions.

> When he was a kid he saw the town through a crack in the grain elevator, an island of trees in the quiet sea of corn. That had been the day the end of the world was at hand. Miss Baumgartner let them out of school so they could go and watch it end, or hide and peek at it from somewhere. Dean Cole and him walked a block and then they ran. They ran all the way to the tracks and down the tracks to the grain elevator, through a hole in the bottom and up the ladder inside. They stretched on their bellies and looked through a crack at the town. They could see all the way to Chapman and a train smoking somewhere. They could see the Platte beyond the tall corn and the bridge where Peewee had dived in the sand, and they could see T. B. Horde driving his county fair mare. They could see it all and the end of the world was at hand.
> The end of the world! he said.
> HOO-RAY! said Dean Cole. [*The Man Who Was There*, p. 116]

Memory's chief contribution to this scene was the mood of apprehension and exhilaration, shared with a companion, on hearing this remarkable news. I recall that school was dismissed, a priceless boon well worth the world's loss. Miss Baumgartner was a borrowed detail, as so many were, from my grade school days in Omaha, where I was all of ten years and more observant.

I did not go up the ladder, as I reported, since I feared all heights more than humiliation. Peewee and the bridge were a cherished rumor at the time of the writing, but the image was generated by the child's exhilaration at the prospect of a mind-boggling disaster. In this brief fiction I gained a shameful triumph over lost time.

Still earlier, from *The Field of Vision*:

> That stovepipe came up through the floor from the coke burner in the room below, and where it bulged like a goiter it would get hot when the damper was down. He could hear the coke crackle and settle when he turned it up. . . . All he wanted to do by turning the damper was to bring up the woman who lived below, the way the genie in the picture would rise out of Aladdin's lamp. She would come up with her lamp, the wick swimming in oil, and cross the room like the figures in his dreams, without noises, without so much as taking steps. Holding the lamp to his face she would see that he was asleep. He would feel the heat of the chimney on his forehead, catch a whiff of the oil. She would first open the damper, then turn with the lamp so that the room darkened behind her, but her snow white hair seemed to trap the light. During the day it would be piled on her head, but when she came up with the lamp it would be in braids. With a silver-handled comb that rattled when she used it, facing the mirror that no longer had a handle, she would comb out the tangled ends of her braids. Out would come, like the burrs in a dog's tail, the knotted hairs. When all the hairs stood up, like a brush, she would pass the ends slowly over the chimney, where they would curl at the tips and crackle with a frying sound. Then the smell, as when she singed a chicken over a hole in the kitchen range, or turned the bird, slowly, in the flame of a cob dipped in kerosene. [*The Field of Vision*, pp. 106–107]

It is difficult for me, sixty years after the event, to penetrate the fiction to memory's fading impression. I lie in bed under a sloping ceiling that seems to smoke and waver with looming, hovering shadows, cast by a lamp.

Out of my sight a woman hums snatches of hymns, as she
brushes her hair. The crackle I hear is made by the
brush. It was on another occasion that I saw her test the
height of the flame in the chimney by stretching one of
her white hairs across the opening at the top. I still fancy
I see its burning glow, like the filament in a light bulb.
This simple scene has the primal elements that stir both
the emotions and the imagination. There is light and
darkness, there is mystery, wonder, and a nameless
apprehension. The moment is ceremonial. My child's
soul is hushed with awe and a tremor of dread as I
anticipate her sonorous prayers. If I attempt to recall
this actual occasion it blows like smoke, yet something
hovers and protects me as if I were cradled at the mouth
of a cave. The details are vague, but the emotion is
inexhaustible.

To what extent is this true of later events, when the
observed details are clearer? In 1958 I visited Mexico,
and spent a memorable week in Matamoros. Six years
later this experience was the basis of a crucial chapter in
One Day, published in 1965. A caged bird is a feature of
Cowie's experience.

A species of canary, Cowie's first impression had been
that it was an object, made of cork and pipe cleaners. Artful,
perhaps. No question it was horrible. There were quills, but
no feathers, below the neck. The head with its lidded eyes
was elevated on the neck like a lampshade. The legs and
claws were twisted bits of wire. Cowie took it as an example
of the Mexican taste for the macabre: the skull-and-bone
cookies eaten by children, the fantastic birds and animals
made out of paper. When he glanced up to see it headless, he
simply thought the head had dropped off. But no. Nothing
lay in the bottom of the cage. The head, with its knife-like
beak, had been tucked under the quills of one wing. Fly it
could not, lacking the feathers. Sing it would not. But on
occasion it hopped. [*One Day,* p. 180]

Mexico is inexhaustibly exotic, at once exhilarating
and harrowing. The sensible and the absurd overlap, the
grotesque is commonplace. For the writer, this garden of
macabre delights is both an inspiration and a disaster. In
admitting to the surreal nature of his impressions, he
must maintain the confidence of the sober reader. My
own disquieting experience in Matamoros featured a
cage without a bird. Gazing at it and through it, over
many days and nights, it became for me a memorably
symbolic object. In Cowie's circumstance it called for a
bird. I imported one I had observed on a previous stay in
Querataro. The perfect setting for both bird and cage
were provided by Matamoros. Cowie's Mexican adventure provided the author with the overview of many
previous visits, arresting and insoluble reflections, that
arise from the dismaying overlapping of extremes that
are both life enhancing and depressing. Without Matamoros none of this would have happened, but little of it
actually occurred in Matamoros. The perfect cage had to
be found for the imaginary bird.

The proliferating image of our time is the photograph.
It is rapidly replacing the "abstraction" as the mirror in
which we seek our multiple selves. Ironically, it was the
photograph that inspired the emergence and triumph of
modern art, freeing the imagination of the artist of his
obsession with appearances. A surfeit of abstractions,
and abstracted sensations, a tonic and inspiration for
half a century, has resulted in a weariness of artifice that
the photograph seems designed to remedy. What else so
instantly confirms our troubled sense of the visible
world? We need the daily reassurance that it exists.
Objects and places, whether coherently grouped or not,
constitute the ambience in which we have our being. The
photograph confirms, the cinema enshrines "the ineluc-
table modality of the visible." That includes its abuses,

the violence that functions as a pornography of sensation. The film has also obscured, momentarily, that its representations, its imitations of life, is an old rather than a new form of image-making, and that the viewer—by a *commodius vicus* of recirculation—is back to the startled point of his departure, the need for further image-making. In the dark cave of the theatre, as under the porch, he must re-imagine what it is he thinks he sees.

Speak, memory, but we are not long in doubt as to who it is that speaks. In this invocation there is a suggestion that memory will speak without intervention. Most writers, as well as readers, would like to think so. It reaffirms our faith in a world that is larger than we are, in a past that truly exists. Are we to accept that memory is the first step in our fiction-making? We do, if the resulting fiction proves to be words. As we now know, language has its own purpose, and distorts in the act of being lucid. To a measurable degree, the more convincing we find the new image the more it has departed from the one remembered. The emotion that fuels the image-making process, and is in turn put to the service of individual talent, departs from the notion that the real world is there to be seized, rather than constructed. It would appear that the primal experience to which God might refer, once we were revealed as naked, and cast out of Eden, is the very experience that is lacking. We are all image-makers, out of necessity. The dreaming cat may have a clearer picture, to his own purpose, than the dreamer in whose lap he curls, but he lacks the faculty of reassembly that distinguishes and terrifies the species homo. Nothing is, but image-making makes it so.

A less sophisticated writer than Nabokov, a frontier plainsman recollecting the frontier experience of his boyhood, dedicates his book to "the most wondrous faculty of memory, God's greatest gift to man."

He is in dead earnest that memory should speak without his willful intervention. He is not disturbed by the problem of transferring memories into language. Confidence of this sort has persuaded most men, including many writers, that memory is an act of repossession free of distortion. No problem arises, in most cases, if the writer is the sole witness to the events described. Here, surely, is the primal experience, rather than one of many wayward impressions. The invention of the photograph gave objective confirmation to the existence of objects, events, and places. We see and document the reality of war. We see planet earth floating above the moon's horizon. This last image is an example of one that exists outside of our abilities to grasp it, in the manner of a religious symbol to which the key emotions are missing.

Before we made fire, before we made tools, we made images. We cannot imagine a time in which we may have lacked imagination. That is what we were, and that is still what we are. In the deep recesses of caves at Lascaux, Altamira, Peche Merle and elsewhere, prehistoric man proved to be an image-maker of baffling sophistication—if we accept the prevalent conception of the pelt-clad primitive of popular science and fiction, a club in one hand, the hair of a female in the other. The ceilings of these caves feature puzzling signs but marvelously clear representations of animals of the hunt. Horses and bisons, the woolly mammoth, the reindeer, are pictured in a manner we think of as "modern." The audacity of the conception is matched by the refinement of execution. Over a gap of twenty thousand years of silence they capture, as we say, our imaginations. We might guess that the artist's talent increased his self-awareness, his sense of uniqueness, distinguishing him from other creatures, this in turn burdening his soul with the enlargement of his sense of wonder. The caves of Lascaux, as well as those near Hannibal, Missouri, in the bluffs along the river, provided refuge for dreamers and image-makers, inscrutably motivated to be more fully conscious. The caveman, the lunatic, the lover, the poet, and the child under the porch, if we can find one, have at their instant disposal the inexhaustible powers of light and darkness, the ceaseless, commonplace, bewildering commingling of memory, emotion, and imagination. That's where it all comes from. Of the making of such fictions there will not soon be an end.

A Biographical Note

Wright Morris was born in Central City, Nebraska, on January 6, 1910, and now makes his home in Mill Valley, California. During the years between he has lived in many parts of the United States and traveled extensively abroad. Morris has been the recipient of three Guggenheim Fellowships (1942, 1947, 1954), of the National Book Award for *The Field of Vision* (1956), of an award from the National Institute of Arts and Letters (1960), and of a grant from the Rockefeller Foundation (1967). He is a member of the National Institute of Arts and Letters and the American Academy of Arts and Sciences. He holds honorary doctorates from Westminster College (Missouri) and the University of Nebraska, both conferred in 1968, and from Pomona College (1973). In 1975 he received the Mari Sandoz Award of the Nebraska Library Association and was elected Honorary Fellow of the Modern Language Association; in 1976 he was named Senior Fellow by the National Endowment for the Humanities. He has lectured at many universities and was a professor of literature at San Francisco State University, where he taught Creative Writing from 1962 until 1975.

A Wright Morris Bibliography

ROBERT L. BOYCE

This listing attempts to include all significant publications by or about Wright Morris and his work through 1975, including dissertations and selected newspaper articles. It encompasses and continues "A Wright Morris Bibliography" by Stanton J. Linden and David Madden, published in the special Wright Morris issue of *Critique* (Winter 1961–62).

The arrangement here is essentially the same as in the Linden and Madden bibliography. The entries are chronological within the following sections:

I. Books by Wright Morris and Reviews of Them
II. Short Stories
III. Articles and Reviews by Wright Morris
IV. Photo-Text Material and Photographs
V. General and Critical Works on Wright Morris
VI. Biographical and Bibliographical Material

Inevitably there is some overlap between these sections: for example, some ostensible reviews are actually critical articles and biographical material appears with many articles by and about Morris.

Thanks are due Jo Morris, David Madden, and the Lincoln, Nebraska, City Libraries for supplying several hard-to-find references. Special thanks go to my two student assistants, Diane Wonka and Jeanne Popelka, for their help. I am, of course, solely responsible for any errors.

I. BOOKS BY WRIGHT MORRIS AND REVIEWS OF THEM

MY UNCLE DUDLEY. New York: Harcourt, Brace and Company, 1942. Westport, Conn.: Greenwood Press, 1970. Lincoln: University of Nebraska Press, 1975 (paperback).

Reviews

Armstrong, Paul. "Philosophic Hobo." *Saturday Review* 25 (11 April 1942): 16.

Hindus, Milton. *New York Herald Tribune Books,* 5 April 1942, p. 10.

"In Brief." *Nation* 154 (4 April 1942): 405.

Marsh, Fred T. "Life on the Road." *New York Times Book Review,* 5 April 1942, pp. 21, 23.

"Try to Figure This One Out." *Lincoln* (Neb.) *Sunday Journal and Star,* 26 April 1942, p. 6C. Review signed "J.S."

THE MAN WHO WAS THERE. New York: Charles Scribner's Sons, 1945.

Reviews

Bell, Lisle. *New York Herald Tribune Weekly Book Review,* 16 December 1945, p. 8.

Bender, R. J. *Chicago Sun Book Week,* 2 December 1945, p. 30.

"Briefly Noted." *New Yorker* 21 (3 November 1945): 101.

Cordell, Richard A. "Was He Really There?" *Saturday Review* 28 (10 November 1945): 41.

Kirkus 13 (15 August 1945): 349.

THE INHABITANTS. New York: Charles Scribner's Sons, 1946. Second edition: New York: Da Capo Press, 1972. Garden City: Amphoto, 1972.

Reviews

Architectural Forum 85 (November 1946): 140.

Butterfield, Roger. "A Spoon River in Photographs." *Saturday Review* 29 (12 October 19460: 29.

Dooley, William Germain. "Rediscovering America." *New York Times Book Review*, 8 September 1946, p. 7.

"From Life." *New York Herald Tribune Book Review*, 12 January 1947, p. 14.

Newhall, Nancy. *Photo League Bulletin*, November 1946, p. 2.

"Reader's List." *New Republic* 115 (11 November 1946): 636.

THE HOME PLACE. New York: Charles Scribner's Sons, 1948. Lincoln: University of Nebraska Press, 1968 (paperback). Gloucester, Mass.: Peter Smith Publisher, 1968.

Reviews

Brenneman, John, "*The Home Place* by Wright Morris." *Nebraska History* 30 (March 1949): 88–89.

"Briefly Noted." *New Yorker* 24 (31 July 1948): 61.

Canby, Courtlandt. "Return to Boyhood with Lens and Pen." *Saturday Review* 31 (24 July 1948): 12.

Dooley, William Germain. "Old Homestead: A Lifelike Montage." *New York Times Book Review*, 18 July 1948, p. 5.

Eaton, Walter Prichard. "House in the Cornfield." *New York Herald Tribune Book Review*, 18 July 1948, p. 4.

Hass, Victor P. "Return to the Old Nebraska 'Home Place'." *Omaha Sunday World-Herald Magazine,* 25 August 1968, p. 31.

"*The Home Place*: Ex-Nebraskan Returns to Picture, Write of Life on Prairie Farm." *Omaha World-Herald Magazine*, 18 July 1948, p. 3C. Excerpts and photos from the book, with comment.

Jackson, Joseph Henry. "A New Fiction Form with Text and

Photos in a Single Story." *San Francisco Chronicle*, 25 July 1948, pp. 10, 12.

————. "This World; Books and Authors the Past Year." *San Francisco Chronicle*, 2 January 1949, p. 12.

Kirkus 16 (15 May 1948): 243.

Library Journal 73 (July 1948): 1027.

Michel, P. *Revue des langues vivantes/Tijdschrift voor levende talen* 37 (1971): 650.

Newhall, Beaumont. "Book Reviews." *Magazine of Art* 42 (March 1949): 112.

"Novel Woven of Dialogs and Photos." *New York Star*, 18 July 1948, p. M 13.

Poore, Charles. "Books of the Times." *New York Times*, 31 July 1948, p. 13.

Price, Emerson. "Masters New Form of Art, Traces Source of Culture." *Cleveland Press*, 3 August 1948, p. 20.

Wisconsin Library Bulletin 44 (October 1948): 165.

Yerxa, Fendall. "Photography Enters New Field: Novel Writing." *New York Herald Tribune*, 25 July 1948, Section V, p. 6.

THE WORLD IN THE ATTIC. New York: Charles Scribner's Sons, 1949. Lincoln: University of Nebraska Press, 1971 (paperback).

Reviews

Booklist 45 (1 July 1949): 366; and 46 (1 September 1949): 14.

"Briefly Noted." *New Yorker* 25 (8 October 1949): 107.

Christian Science Monitor, 12 January 1950, p. 11.

Davis, Kenneth S. "Nostalgia and Nausea." *Saturday Review* 32 (24 September 1949): 19.

Harrison, W. K. *Library Journal* 74 (August 1949): 1095.

Hass, Victor P. "Hometown Revisited: Was It Nostalgia or Nausea He Felt?" *Omaha Sunday World-Herald Magazine*, 28 August 1949, p. 25C.

Kirkus 17 (15 July 1949): 368.

McNaught, Eleanor. *Canadian Forum* 29 (December 1949): 214–15.

Parsons, Elizabeth. "Stopover in a Nebraska Town." *New York Times Book Review*, 28 August 1949, p. 4.

Ross, Mary. "Whistle Stop Revisited." *New York Herald Tribune Book Review*, 28 August 1949, p. 6.

MAN AND BOY. New York: Alfred A. Knopf, 1951. Toronto: McClelland and Stewart, 1951. London: Victor Gollancz, 1952. Turin, Italy: Einaudi, 1954. Lincoln: University of Nebraska Press, 1974 (paperback).

Reviews

Booklist 47 (1 July 1951): 381.

Bookmark 10 (July 1951): 232.

Butcher, Fanny. *Chicago Sunday Tribune*, 27 May 1951, p. 5.

Jackson, Joseph Henry. *San Francisco Chronicle*, 12 June 1951, p. 14.

Kirkus 19 (15 March 1951): 163.

Library Journal 76 (15 March 1951): 862.

Little, Carl Victor. "Mother—Phoeey & Viva." *Saturday Review* 34 (2 June 1951): 13–14.

Longstreth, T. M. *Christian Science Monitor*, 14 June 1951, p. 15.

Morris, Alice S. "Mother Ormsby's Iron Apron Strings." *New York Times Book Review*, 20 May 1951, p. 4.

Phelps, Robert. "Fiction Parade." *New Republic* 125 (23 July 1951): 21.

Pickrel, Paul. "Outstanding Novels," *Yale Review* 40 (Summer 1951): 767.

Prescott, Orville. "Books of the Times." *New York Times*, 30 May 1951, p. 21.

Sugrue, Thomas. "Tragi-comedy of an Unbeatable Mother." *New York Herald Tribune Book Review*, 20 May 1951, p. 6.

Swados, Harvey. "Gothic and Some 'Fellers'." *Nation* 173 (16 June 1951): 571.

"The Weak and the Strong." *Time* 57 (28 May 1951): 110.

West, Anthony. "Books." *New Yorker* 27 (16 June 1951): 95–96.

THE WORKS OF LOVE. New York: Alfred A. Knopf, 1952. Lincoln: University of Nebraska Press, 1972 (paperback). Reprinted in *Wright Morris: A Reader*. New York: Harper and Row, 1970.

Reviews

Booklist 48 (15 March 1952): 229.

"Books in Brief." *New Republic* 126 (26 May 1952): 21.

"Briefly Noted." *New Yorker* 28 (23 February 1952): 107.

Butcher, Fanny. *Chicago Sunday Tribune*, 24 February 1952, p. 4.

Dedmon, Emmett. "Emotional Drifting." *Saturday Review* 35 (15 March 1952): 33.

Hicks, Granville. "A Chronicle of Current Fiction." *New Leader* 35 (24 March 1952): 20. Reprinted in Granville Hicks. *Literary Horizons: A Quarter Century of American Fiction*, pp. 9–10. New York: New York University Press, 1970.

Hughes, Riley. "New Novels." *Catholic World* 175 (April 1952): 75.

Kirkus 19 (15 December 1951): 711.

McGovern, Hugh. "Wright Morris's New Novel." *New York Herald Tribune Book Review*, 13 April 1952, p. 10.

Madden, David. *Richmond* (Va.) *Mercury Book Review*, 6 December 1972, p. 12.

Sullivan, Richard. "Questing and Drifting." *New York Times Book Review*, 2 March 1952, p. 4.

Swados, Harvey. "Man Alone." *Nation* 174 (14 June 1952): 587.

"That Lonesome Road." *Time* 59 (10 March 1952): 112.

THE DEEP SLEEP. New York: Charles Scribner's Sons, 1953. London: Eyre and Spottiswoode, 1954. Stuttgart, Germany: Goverts, 1957. Frankfurt, Germany: Fischer Bucherei, 1960 (paperback). Milan, Italy: Arnoldo Mondadori, 1961. Frankfurt, Germany: Suhrkamp, 1967 (paperback). Lincoln: University of Nebraska Press, 1975 (paperback).

Reviews

Aldridge, John W. "Heart of a Secret Tragedy." *New York Times Book Review*, 13 September 1953, pp. 4–5.

Booklist 50 (15 September 1953): 35.

"Briefly Noted." *New Yorker* 29 (19 September 1953): 118.

Gebsattel, Jerôme von. "The Deep Sleep." *Kindlers Literatur Lexikon*, pp. 2413–14. Zurich: Kindler Verlag, 1970.

Harding, Walter. *Chicago Sunday Tribune*, 1 November 1953, p. 3.

Hicks, Granville, "Two New Novels of Life's Mystery by Wright Morris and Saul Bellow." *New Leader* 36 (21 September 1953): 23–24. Reprinted in Granville Hicks. *Literary Horizons: A Quarter Century of American Fiction*, pp. 11–13. New York: New York University Press, 1970.

Jackson, Joseph Henry. *San Francisco Chronicle*, 24 September 1953, p. 15.

Kirkus 21 (15 June 1953): 370.

Library Journal. 78 (1 September 1953): 1425.

Murray, William. "Helpless Pawn." *Saturday Review* 36 (19 September 1953): 16.

Pickrel, Paul, "Outstanding Novels." *Yale Review* 43 (Autumn 1953): 8.

Raleigh, John Henry. "Four New Novels." *New Republic* 129 (14 December 1953): 21.

Scott, Eleanor M. "Quiet Desperation in a Comfortable Middle-Class Home." *New York Herald Tribune Book Review*, 13 September 1953, p. 2.

"The September Glut." *Time* 62 (21 September 1953); 114.

Weiss, Carol H. "Household Detail." *Commentary* 16 (16 October 1953): 45.

THE HUGE SEASON. New York: The Viking Press, 1954. London: Secker and Warburg, 1955. Stuttgart, Germany: Goverts, 1958. New York: Pyramid Books, 1969 (paperback). Lincoln: University of Nebraska Press, 1975 (paperback).

Reviews

Booklist 51 (15 September 1954): 30.

Butcher, Fanny. *Chicago Sunday Tribune*, 3 October 1954, p. 4.

Cooperman, Stanley. "Time in Modern Fiction." *Nation* 179 (16 October 1954): 344.

Fussell, Edwin. "The Mid-Fifties Novel." *Western Review* 19 (Summer 1955): 297–308.

Hicks, Granville. "Wright Morris's New Novel Contrasts the World of the '20s and the '50s." *New Leader* 37 (4 October 1954): 21–22. Reprinted in Granville Hicks. *Literary Horizons: A Quarter Century of American Fiction*, pp. 13–18. New York: New York University Press, 1970.

Kirkus 22 (15 August 1954): 543.

Library Journal 79 (1 October 1954): 1825.

"Mixed Fiction." *Time* 64 (25 October 1954): 92.

Mizener, Arthur. "Of the 20's and Later." *New York Herald Tribune Book Review*, 10 October 1954, p. 8.

Mudrick, Marvin. "Humanity is the Principle." *Hudson Review* 7 Winter 1955): 610–11.

Pickrel, Paul. "Outstanding Fiction." *Yale Review* 44 (Winter 1955): 317.

Prescott, Orville. "Books of the Times." *New York Times,* 1 October 1954, p. 21.

Quinn, Patrick F. "That Endless Weekend." *Commonweal* 61 (22 October 1954): 72.

Schorer, Mark. "Past Captives, Present Pawns." *New York Times Book Review*, 3 October 1954, p. 4.

Webster, Harvey Curtis. "Journey Between Two Eras." *Saturday Review* 37 (2 October 1954); 29.

West, Anthony. "The Huge Season." *New Yorker* 30 (9 October 1954): 175.

THE FIELD OF VISION. New York: Harcourt, Brace and Company, 1956. New York: New American Library, 1957 (paperback). London: Weidenfeld and Nicolson, 1957. Milan, Italy: Feltrinelli, 1962. Lincoln: University of Nebraska Press, 1974 (paperback). Japanese edition, 1974. Reprinted in *Wright Morris: A Reader.* New York: Harper and Row, 1970.

Reviews

Aldridge, John W. "Prisoners of the Past," *New York Times Book Review*, 30 September 1956, p. 5.

Allen, Walter. "New Stories and Novels." *New Statesman*, 7 September 1957, p. 294.

Bookmark 16 (November 1956): 37.

DeMott, Benjamin. "Agonists and Agonizers, and a Utopian." *Hudson Review* 10 (Spring 1957): 140–48.

"Durable Fragments." *Newsweek* 48 (1 October 1956): 94.

Fiedler, Leslie. "Some Footnotes on the Fiction of '56." *Reporter* 15 (13 December 1956): 44–46.

Gebsattel, Jerôme von. "The Field of Vision." *Kindlers Literatur Lexikon*, pp. 3507–8. Zurich: Kindler Verlag, 1970.

Gill, Brendan. "Books." *New Yorker* 32 (17 November 1956): 236.

Hartman, Carl. "Mr. Morris and Others." *Western Review* 21 (Summer 1957): 307–9.

Hass, Victor P. "Bullfight Evokes Curious Memories." *Chicago Sunday Tribune, Magazine of Books*, 7 October 1956, p. 3.

Hayes, E. Nelson. "Recent Fiction." *Progressive* 21 (February 1957): 35.

Hicks, Granville. "Living With Books; 'The Field of Vision' by Wright Morris a Significant and Enriching Novel." *New Leader* 39 (1 October 1956): 24–25. Reprinted in Granville Hicks. *Literary Horizons: A Quarter Century of American Fiction*, pp. 18–23. New York: New York University Press, 1970.

———. "Living with Books; C. P. Snow's 'Homecoming' Describes Social as Well as Individual Problems." *New Leader* 39 (22 October 1956): 24–25.

Hopkinson, Tom. "New Novels." *Observer*, 25 August 1957, p. 13.

Kirkus 24 (15 July 1956): 495.

Madden, David. *Masterplots*. Comprehensive Library Edition; The Four Series in Eight Volumes, pp. 1591–94. New York: Salem Press, 1968.

"Mixed Fiction." *Time* 68 (15 October 1956): 126.

Patterson, Jack. "Heroic Act to Sterile Gesture." *Commonweal* 65 (9 November 1956): 156.

Poore, Charles. "Books of the Times." *New York Times*, 27 September 1956, p. 33.

Rideout, Walter B. "Introspection in the Bull Ring," *Chicago Sun-Times*, 7 October 1956, Section VIII, p. 2.

San Francisco Chronicle, 25 November 1956, p. 30.

Scott, Winfield Townley. "Ring Around a Hero," *Saturday Review* 39 (6 October 1956): 24.

Stringer, Ann. "Reading for Pleasure; Clear Images." *Wall Street Journal*, 18 October 1956, p. 12.

Walsh, Chad. "According to Their Lights, If and When They Come On." *New York Herald Tribune Book Review*, 7 October 1956, p. 6.

LOVE AMONG THE CANNIBALS. New York: Harcourt, Brace and Company, 1957. New York: New American Library, 1958 (paperback). London: Weidenfeld and Nicolson, 1958. Milan, Italy: Feltrinelli, 1958. Stuttgart, Germany: Goverts, 1959. Rio de Janeiro: Editora Vecchi, 1960. Frankfurt, Germany: Fischer Bucherei, 1962. Toronto: New American Library of Canada, 1963 (paperback). Milan, Italy: Garzanti, 1966.

Reviews

Adams, Phoebe. "Reader's Choice." *Atlantic Monthly* 200 (September 1957): 85.

Bensen, Donald R. "Dream Girl Revisited." *Saturday Review* 40 (17 August 1957): 14.

"Briefly Noted." *New Yorker* 33 (24 August 1957): 109.

Butcher, Fanny. *Chicago Sunday Tribune*, 11 August 1957, p. 2.

Davis, Richard Gorham. "Encounter With a Pagan Goddess." *New York Times Book Review*, 11 August 1957, p. 4.

Hicks, Granville. "Wright Morris Turns to Sex in His 11th Novel, 'Love Among the Cannibals.'" *New Leader* 40 (19 August 1957): 21–22. Reprinted in Granville Hicks. *Literary Horizons: A Quarter Century of American Fiction*, pp. 23–28. New York: New York University Press, 1970.

Hogan, William. *San Francisco Chronicle*, 8 August 1957, p. 21.

Kirkus 25 (1 June 1957): 395.

Library Journal 82 (1 September 1957): 2039.

"Mixed Fiction." *Time* 70 (19 August 1957): 82.

Poore, Charles, "Books of the Times." *New York Times*, 8 August 1957, p. 21.

Price, Martin. "In the Fielding Country: Some Recent Fiction." *Yale Review* 47 (Autumn 1957): 151.

Rogers, W. G. "Nebraskan Writes Gay, Masterly New Comedy." *Lincoln* (Neb.) *Sunday Journal and Star*, 4 August 1957, p. 2D.

Scott, Winfield Townley. "Wright Morris Tries a Satiric Comedy." *New York Herald Tribune Book Review*, 11 August 1957, p. 7.

Stevenson, David L. "Minor Rebellions." *Nation* 185 (12 October 1957): 248.

THE TERRITORY AHEAD. New York: Harcourt, Brace and Company, 1958. New York, Atheneum, 1963 (paperback). Toronto: McClelland and Stewart, 1963. 1963 printings include "One Law for the Lion" as a "Postscript."

Reviews

Becket, Roger. "Their Subjects Wait Within." *New York Herald Tribune Book Review*, 18 January 1959, p. 4.

Booklist 55 (1 December 1958): 179.

Bookmark 18 (November 1958): 33.

Harding, Walter. *Chicago Sunday Tribune*, 2 November 1958, p. 3.

Haselton, Stephen J. *Thought, Fordham University Quarterly* 35 (Autumn 1960): 467–68.

Hicks, Granville. "Wright Morris as Critic." *Saturday Review* 41 (25 October 1958): 14. Reprinted in Granville Hicks. *Literary Horizons: A Quarter Century of American Fiction*, pp. 28–31. New York: New York University Press, 1970.

Kirkus 26 (15 July 1958): 537.

Library Journal 83 (1 September 1958): 2308.

Millar, Kenneth. *San Francisco Chronicle*, 28 December 1958, p. 15.

Podhoretz, Norman. "The Flight from Aunt Sally." *Reporter* 19 (27 November 1958): 39–40.

Rolo, Charles. "The Peripatetic Reviewer." *Atlantic Monthly* 202 (December 1958): 90.

Ward, J. W. "In Brief." *Nation* 188 (24 January 1959): 75.

CEREMONY IN LONE TREE. New York: Atheneum, 1960. Don Mills, Ontario: Longmans, Green and Company, 1960. London: Weidenfeld and Nicolson, 1961. New York: New American Library, 1962 (paperback). Toronto: New American Library of Canada, 1962 (paperback). Munich, Germany: Piper Verlag, 1962. Milan, Italy: Feltrinelli, 1962. Paris, France: Gallimard, 1964 (cloth, paperback). Buenos Aires: Plaza & Janes, 1967. Lincoln: University of Nebraska Press, 1973 (paperback).

Reviews

Adams, Phoebe. "Reader's Choice." *Atlantic Monthly* 206 (July 1960): 98.

Booklist 56 (15 July 1960): 682.

Bookmark 19 (July 1960): 261.

Cosman, Max. "The Relentless Wheel of Nature." *Commonweal* 72 (5 August 1960): 404.

deFord, Miriam Allen. *Humanist* 21 (March–April 1961): 124.

DeMott, Benjamin. "Fiction Chronicle." *Partisan Review* 27 (Fall 1960): 754–59.

Didion, Joan. "Notes From a Summer Reader." *National Review* 8 (10 September 1960): 152.

Engle, Paul. "Myth Out of Reality." *New York Times Book Review,* 10 July 1960, p. 5.

Gardiner, Harold C. "Story Needed." *America* 103 (23 July 1960): 481–82.

Gebsattel, Jerôme von. "Ceremony in Lone Tree." *Kindlers Literatur Lexikon,* p. 1869. Zurich: Kindler Verlag, 1970.

Gorn, L. H. "Innocence Is at the Core of the Most Worldly." *San Francisco Chronicle, This World* Magazine, 7 August 1960, p. 18.

Hass, Victor P. *Chicago Sunday Tribune,* 10 July 1960, Pt. 4, p. 10.

"Haunting Reunion." *Newsweek* 56 (11 July 1960): 94.

Hicks, Granville. "Landscape of the Lonesome Plains." *Saturday Review* 43 (9 July 1960): 11. Reprinted in Granville Hicks. *Literary Horizons: A Quarter Century of American Fiction,* pp. 32–35. New York: New York University Press, 1970.

Hines, E. E. "Morris Novel Proves Ex-Nebraskan is Acute Observer of Rural Scene." *Lincoln* (Neb.) *Sunday Journal and Star,* 10 July 1960, p. 9B.

Hollander, John. "Plan and Fancy: Notes on Four Novels." *Yale Review* 50 (Autumn 1960): 155.

Kirkus 28 (1 May 1960): 359.

Madden, David. *Masterplots.* Comprehensive Library Edition, The Four Series in Eight Volumes, pp. 672–75. New York: Salem Press, 1968.

Masterplots 1961 *Annual,* pp. 33–35. New York: Salem Press, 1961. Reprinted in *Survey of Contemporary Literature,* ed. Frank N. Magill, vol. I: 670–72. New York: Salem Press, 1971.

Mercier, Vivian. "Sex, Success, and Salvation." *Hudson Review* 13 (Autumn 1960): 449.

Mitgang, Herbert. "Books of the Times." *New York Times,* 11 July 1960, p. 27.

"Mixed Fiction." *Time* 76 (11 July 1960): 104.

"Notes on Current Books." *Virginia Quarterly Review* 37 (Winter 1961): viii.

Oboler, Eli M. *Library Journal* 85 (15 May 1960): 1937.

Pickrel, Paul. "The New Books." *Harper's Magazine* 221 (August 1960): 96.

Publishers' Weekly 203 (26 February 1973): 125.

Southern, Terry. "New Trends and Old Hats." *Nation* 191 (19 November 1960): 380.

Tornquist, Elizabeth. "The New Parochialism." *Commentary* 31 (May 1961): 449.

Walsh, Chad. "Wright Morris' Novel of a Time-Ridden Nebraska Clan." *New York Herald Tribune Book Review,* 10 July 1960, p. 5.

"Without Benefit of Story." *Times Literary Supplement,* 10 March 1961, p. 149.

THE MISSISSIPPI RIVER READER. Edited by Wright Morris. Garden City: Doubleday and Company (Anchor Books), 1962 (paperback).

WHAT A WAY TO GO. New York: Atheneum, 1962. Munich, Germany: Piper Verlag, 1964.

Reviews

Adams, Phoebe. "Greece Anyone?" *Atlantic Monthly* 210 (October 1962): 146–47.

"Back to the Body." *Newsweek* 60 (1 October 1962): 83.

Beck, Warren. *Chicago Sunday Tribune,* 7 October 1962, p. 5.

Booth, Wayne C. "Professor Soby's Sabbatical." *New York Times Book Review,* 23 September 1962, p. 4.

"Briefly Noted." *New Yorker* 38 (20 October 1962): 230.

DeMott, Benjamin. "The New Books." *Harper's Magazine* 225 (October 1962): 94.

Griffin, L. W. *Library Journal* 87 (1 August 1962): 2777.

Hassan, Ihab. "Confetti for Bacchanalia." *Saturday Review* 45 (22 September 1962): 30, 35.

Hogan, William. *San Francisco Chronicle*, 1 October 1962, p. 49.

Jonas, Gerald. *New York Herald Tribune Books*, 14 October 1962, p. 10.

Kirkus 30 (1 July 1962): 643.

Levine, Paul. "The Season's Difference." *Hudson Review* 15 (Winter 1962–63): 601–2.

"Love in Venice." *Time* 80 (21 September 1962): 94, 96.

Madden, David. "The Finest Craftsman." *Shenandoah* 14 (Autumn 1962): 58–60.

Madden, David. *Masterplots* 1963 *Annual*, pp. 290–94. New York, Salem Press, 1963. Reprinted in *Survey of Contemporary Literature*, ed. Frank N. Magill, vol. 7: 5008–12. New York: Salem Press, 1971.

Maddocks, Melvin. "Morris's Prufrock." *Christian Science Monitor*, 20 September 1962, p. 11.

"Notes on Current Books." *Virginia Quarterly Review* 39 (Winter 1963): x.

CAUSE FOR WONDER. New York: Atheneum, 1963. Toronto: McClelland and Stewart, 1963.

Reviews

Adams, Robert M. "Three Novels." *New York Review of Books*, 14 November 1963, pp. 12–13.

Barrett, William. "Novelists Testing . . . Testing." *Atlantic Monthly* 212 (November 1963): 148, 150.

Baumbach, Jonathan. *Masterplots* 1964 *Annual*, pp. 49–51. New York: Salem Press, 1964. Reprinted in *Survey of Contemporary Literature*, ed. Frank N. Magill, vol. 1: 655–57. New York: Salem Press, 1971.

Bush, Geoffrey. "Some Recent Fiction." *Yale Review* 53 (Winter 1964): 299–300.

Dumas, R. H. *Library Journal* 88 (1 October 1963): 3646.

"Ghost Story." *Newsweek* 62 (23 September 1963): 106, 108.

Harnack, Curtis. *Chicago Sunday Tribune, Magazine of Books*, 29 September 1963, p. 10.

"Horsebackwards." *Time* 82 (4 October 1963): 126, 128.

Madden, David. "E = MC²." *Saturday Review* 46 (21 September 1963): 36.

"Notes on Current Books." *Virginia Quarterly Review* 40 (Winter 1964): viii–ix.

Poore, Charles. "An Acrid Comedy of Growing Old." *New York Times*, 19 September 1963, p. 25.

Sale, Roger. "The Newness of the Novel." *Hudson Review* 16 (Winter 1963–64): 606–7.

Scott, Winfield Townley. *Book Week*, 6 October 1963, p. 6.

Stevenson, David L. "Americans in a Place Not Their Own." *New York Times Book Review*, 22 September 1963, p. 5. Accompanied by remarks by Wright Morris.

ONE DAY. New York: Atheneum, 1965. Toronto: McClelland and Stewart, 1965.

Reviews

"Also Current." *Time* 85 (26 March 1965): 104.

Barrett, William. "The Banal and the Beautiful." *Atlantic Monthly* 215 (April 1965): 154–56.

Bergonzi, Bernard. "New Novels." *New York Review of Books*, 11 March 1965, p. 20.

Berolzheimer, H. F. *Library Journal* 90 (15 April 1965): 1933.

Booth, Wayne C. *Kenyon Review* 27 (Summer 1965): 569–70.

Choice 2 (July–August 1965): 299.

Dayle, P. A. *Best Sellers* 24 (1 March 1965): 469.

Donadio, Stephen. "The Day That Was." *Partisan Review* 32 (Summer 1965): 466–68.

"Escondido, Nov. 22, 1963." *Newsweek* 65 (22 February 1965): 97–98.

Green, Howard. "The Countess' Hat." *Hudson Review* 18 (Summer 1965): 284–85.

Hicks, Granville. "Time Stops and the World Goes On." *Saturday Review* 48 (20 February 1965): 23–24. Reprinted in Granville Hicks. *Literary Horizons: A Quarter Century of American Fiction,* pp. 35–40. New York: New York University Press, 1970.

Hill, William B. "Books to Be Noted . . . 1965: Fiction." *America* 112 (8 May 1965): 677–78.

Howard, Richard. *Book Week,* 21 March 1965, p. 4.

Jackson, Katherine Gauss. "Books in Brief." *Harper's Magazine* 230 (May 1965): 145–46.

Klein, Marcus. "Love Among the Artifacts." *Reporter* 32 (8 April 1965): 53–54.

Kozol, Jonathan. " 'One Day': Too Many Moments." *Christian Science Monitor,* 25 February 1965, p. 7.

Madden, David. *Masterplots 1966 Annual,* pp. 213–18. New York: Salem Press, 1967. Reprinted in *Survey of Contemporary Literature,* ed. Frank N. Magill, vol. 5: 3412–17. New York: Salem Press, 1971.

Miller, Warren. *Commonweal* 81 (12 March 1965): 769.

Murray, James G. "The Day Before Saturday." *Critic* 23 (April–May 1965): 79–80.

"Notes On Current Books." *Virginia Quarterly Review* 41 (Summer 1965): lxxxi.

Poore, Charles. "A Novel of Americans on a Fateful Day in History." *New York Times,* 23 February 1965, p. 31.

Stevenson, David L. "What Was It Like To Be Oneself?" *New York Times Book Review,* 7 March 1965, pp. 4, 32.

IN ORBIT. New York: New American Library, 1967 (cloth), 1968 (paperback). Don Mills, Ontario: General Publishing Company, 1967.

Reviews

Bannon, Barbara A. *Publishers' Weekly* 190 (12 December 1966): 48–49.

Cook, Roderick. "Books in Brief." *Harper's Magazine* 234 (March 1967): 139.

Edelstein, A. *National Observer*, 20 March 1967, p. 21.

"Empty Circles." *Time* 89 (17 February 1967): 104.

Fremont-Smith, Eliot. "Motorcycle Misfits—Fiction and Fact." *New York Times*, 23 February 1967, p. 4.

Hass, Victor P. *Books Today* 4 (19 February 1967): 10.

Hicks, Granville. "Huck Finn on a Motorcycle." *Saturday Review* 50 (18 February 1967): 29–30. Reprinted in Granville Hicks. *Literary Horizons: A Quarter Century of American Fiction*, pp. 40–43, New York: New York University Press, 1970.

Howard, Maureen. "Other Voices." *Partisan Review* 35 (Winter 1968): 146–47.

Kirkus 34 (15 December 1966): 1298.

Kohn, Marjorie. *Library Journal* 92 (1 February 1967): 596.

Kriegel, Leonard. *Commonweal* 86 (7 April 1967): 98.

Peterson, C. *Book World*, 23 June 1968, p. 13.

Phillips, Robert. *North American Review* 252 (May 1967): 40.

Phillipson, J. S. *Best Sellers* 26 (15 February 1967): 409.

Publishers' Weekly 193 (13 May 1968): 61.

Rogers, Thomas. *Book Week*, 19 February 1967, p. 4.

Wain, John. "Versions of Pastoral." *New York Review of Books*, 4 May 1967, p. 36.

Walker, Gerald. "A Happening." *New York Times Book Review*, 5 February 1967, p. 44.

Weeks, Edward. "Spaceman At Large." *Atlantic Monthly* 219 (April 1967): 144.

A BILL OF RITES, A BILL OF WRONGS, A BILL OF GOODS. New York: New American Library, 1968. Don Mills, Ontario: General Publishing Company, 1968.

Reviews

Berek, Peter. "Bills Past Due." *Nation* 206 (8 April 1968): 478–79.

Christian Century 85 (28 February 1968): 268.

Hicks, Granville. "Sounds of an Uneasy Artist." *Saturday Review* 51 (16 March 1968): 29–30. Reprinted in Granville Hicks. *Literary Horizons: A Quarter Century of American Fiction*, pp. 43–46. New York: New York University Press, 1970.

McKenzie, J. L. *National Observer*, 13 May 1968, p. 21.
Maddocks, Melvin. *Christian Science Monitor*, 14 March 1968, p. 12.
Publishers' Weekly 192 (25 December 1967): 51.
Simon, John. "A Table of Contempts." *New York Times Book Review*, 14 July 1968, pp. 12, 14.
Wagenknecht, T. M. *Library Journal* 93 (15 January 1968): 201.
Wolff, Geoffrey. *Book World*, 2 June 1968, p. 14.

GOD'S COUNTRY AND MY PEOPLE. New York: Harper and Row, 1968.

Reviews

Adams, Phoebe. "Short Reviews: Books." *Atlantic Monthly* 223 (January 1969): 118.
Bridges, Les. *Book World*, 8 December 1968, p. 10.
Christian Science Monitor, 29 November 1968, p. B3.
Coles, Robert. "Books." *New Yorker* 45 (18 October 1969): 205–6, 209–13.
Jackson, Katherine Gauss. "Books in Brief." *Harper's Magazine* 238 (January 1969): 105.
Lask, Thomas. "End Papers." *New York Times*, 26 February 1969, p. 45.
Showers, Paul. *New York Times Book Review*, 8 December 1968, p. 64.
Weiss, Margaret R. "With A Camera Eye on Christmas." *Saturday Review* 51 (30 November 1968): 55.
Wright, T. W. *Library Journal* 94 (1 February 1969): 564.

WRIGHT MORRIS: A READER. Introduction by Granville Hicks. New York: Harper and Row, 1970. Toronto: Fitzhenry and Whiteside, 1970. New York: Avon, 1974 (paperback).

Wright Morris included in this anthology *The Works of Love*, *The Field of Vision*, "The Ram in the Thicket," and "The Safe Place," in their entirety, and selections from the following books: *Cause for Wonder, Ceremony in Lone Tree, The Deep*

Sleep, Love Among the Cannibals, My Uncle Dudley, One Day, The Territory Ahead, and *The World in the Attic.*
Reviews
Booth, Wayne C. "My Granpa's Scalp." *Nation* 210 (23 March 1970): 344–45.
Griffin, L. W. *Library Journal* 94 (1 October 1969): 3468.
Kuehl, Linda. "Frontiersman By His Own Intent." *Christian Science Monitor,* 19 March 1970, p. 17.
Lehmann-Haupt, C. "It's Not So Minor To Be Minor." *New York Times,* 5 January 1970, p. 35.
Madden, David. "A Neglected Seer." *New Republic* 162 (10 January 1970): 28–30.
Pritchard, William H. "Senses of Reality." *Hudson Review* 23 (Spring 1970): 167–68.
Wolff, Geoffrey. "Transforming the Past." *Newsweek* 75 (12 January 1970): 70, 72.

GREEN GRASS, BLUE SKY, WHITE HOUSE. Los Angeles: Black Sparrow Press, 1970 (cloth, paperback).

Reprinted here are "Since When Do They Charge Admission," "Drrdla," and "Green Grass, Blue Sky, White House."
Reviews
Griffin, L. W. *Library Journal* 96 (15 February 1971): 657.
Mudrick, Marvin. "Scrupulous Permutations and Occult Resemblances." *Hudson Review* 24 (Spring 1971): 187–89.

FIRE SERMON. New York: Harper and Row, 1971. Toronto: Fitzhenry and Whiteside, 1971. Greenwich, Connecticut: Fawcett Publications, Inc., 1975 (Ladder Edition).
Reviews
Booklist 68 (15 October 1971): 183.
"Briefly Noted." *New Yorker* 47 (18 September 1971): 142.
Carver, W. "A Silk Purse and a Sow's Ear." *Carleton Miscellany* 12 (Fall–Winter 1971–72): 151.
Choice 8 (January 1972): 1454.

Cooper, Arthur. *Newsweek* 78 (25 October 1971): 120.

Ferguson, Linda W. "Or Did Morris Write the Great One?" *Pacific Sun,* 29 September 1971, p. 11.

Folsom, James K. *Western American Literature* 7 (Spring 1972): 72–73.

Foote, A. C. *Book World,* 19 September 1971, p. 2.

Griffin, L. W. *Library Journal* 96 (1 August 1971): 2544.

Hass, Victor P. "Native Son's Finest Novel." *Omaha Sunday World-Herald Magazine,* 22 August 1971, p. 22.

Hicks, Granville. "Floyd and Kermit at the Crossroads." *New York Times Book Review,* 26 September 1971, pp. 52–53.

Kirkus 39 (15 June 1971): 653.

Madden, David. "The Master Nods." *Shenandoah* 24 (Fall 1972): 81–84.

National Observer, 25 September 1971, p. 21.

Publishers' Weekly 199 (7 June 1971): 50.

Rooke, Constance. *Malahat Review,* No. 21 (January 1972): 117.

Rynne, Diane. *Library Journal* 96 (15 December 1971): 4206.

Seelye, John. "Novel #16." *New Republic* 165 (30 October 1971): 23–24.

Stern, Daniel. *Life Magazine* 71 (27 August 1971): 14.

Van Brunt, H. L. "The Headiest, Happiest Holiday Gifts: Books." *Saturday Review* 54 (27 November 1971): 46.

Virginia Quarterly Review 48 (Winter 1972): xvi.

Walters, Thomas N. *Masterplots* 1972 *Annual,* pp. 145–49. Englewood Cliffs, New Jersey: Salem Press, 1972.

Weales, Gerald. "Fiction Chronicle." *Hudson Review* 24 (Winter 1971–72): 725–26.

Weeks, Edward. "The Peripatetic Reviewer." *Atlantic Monthly* 228 (September 1971): 115.

Wernick, Robert. "Remembrance of Cranks Past." *Time* 98 (18 October 1971): 88–89.

LOVE AFFAIR—A VENETIAN JOURNAL. New York: Harper and Row, 1972.

Reviews

Best Sellers 32 (1 November 1972): 356.

Booklist 69 (1 January 1973): 426.
"Briefly Noted." *New Yorker* 48 (11 November 1972): 191.
Christian Century 89 (22 November 1972): 1187.
Donohue, J. W. *America* 127 (21 October 1972): 327.
Hass, Victor P. "Wright Morris Writes Journal About Life In A Lovely City." *Omaha Sunday World-Herald Magazine,* 22 October 1972, p. 31.
Herman, Dick. "Eiseley & Morris." *Lincoln* (Neb.) *Sunday Journal and Star. Focus,* 29 April 1973, p. 23H.
Kirkus 40 (15 August 1972): 1018.
Saturday Review 55 (7 October 1972): 108.
World 1 (19 December 1972): 67.

WAR GAMES. Los Angeles: Black Sparrow Press, 1972 (cloth, paperback).
Reviews
Griffin, L. W. *Library Journal* 97 (15 June 1972): 2200.
"Notes on Current Books." *Virginia Quarterly Review* 48 (Summer 1972): xcviii.
Rooke, Constance. *Malahat Review,* No. 23 (July 1972): 143–44.

A LIFE. New York: Harper and Row, 1973. Toronto: Fitzhenry and Whiteside, 1973.
Reviews
Bannon, Barbara A. *Publishers' Weekly* 204 (9 July 1973): 41.
Booklist 70 (15 January 1974): 517.
Broyard, Anatole. "Octogenarian at the Wheel." *New York Times,* 23 August 1973, p. 35.
Choice 10 (January 1974): 1719.
Dillard, R. H. W. *Masterplots* 1974 *Annual,* pp. 229–32. Englewood Cliffs, New Jersey: Salem Press, 1975.
Ferguson, Linda W. "Wright Morris Talks About A Return." *Pacific Sun,* 1 November 1973, p. 32. Includes remarks by Wright Morris.
Griffin, L. W. *Library Journal* 98 (15 September 1973): 2572.

Hislop, Alan. *Book World,* 14 October 1973, p. 6.

Kirkus 41 (1 July 1973): 710.

Koltz, Newton. "Floyd Warner, Raging Old Man." *New York Times Book Review,* 26 August 1973, p. 6.

National Observer, 22 September 1973, p. 23.

"1973: A Selection of Noteworthy Titles." *New York Times Book Review,* 2 December 1973, p. 76.

"Notes On Current Books." *Virginia Quarterly Review* 50 (Winter 1974): viii.

Rabinowitz, Dorothy. "Books in Brief." *Saturday Review/World* 1 (9 October 1973): 28.

Weeks, Edward. "The Peripatetic Reviewer." *Atlantic Monthly* 232 (September 1973): 116–17.

Wernick, Robert. "Gold and Grit." *Time* 102 (24 September 1973): 126.

HERE IS EINBAUM. Los Angeles: Black Sparrow Press, 1973 (cloth, paperback).

Reprinted here are "Here Is Einbaum," "Magic," "A Fight Between a White Boy and a Black Boy in the Dusk of a Fall Afternoon in Omaha, Nebraska," "Fiona," and "In Another Country."

Reviews

Choice 10 (January 1974): 1719.

"Notes on Current Books." *Virginia Quarterly Review* 50 (Winter 1974): x.

ABOUT FICTION: REVERENT REFLECTIONS ON THE NATURE OF FICTION WITH IRREVERENT OBSERVATIONS ON WRITERS, READERS, AND OTHER ABUSES. New York: Harper and Row, 1975.

Reviews

Angell, Joseph W. "Wright Morris Discusses Fiction." *Prairie Schooner* 49 (Summer 1975): 166–68.

Booklist 71 (1 March 1975): 665.

Choice 12 (May 1975): 386.

Cushman, Keith. *Library Journal* 100 (1 January 1975): 53.

Kirkus 42 (1 November 1974): 1190.

Madden, David. *AWP* (Associated Writing Programs) *Newsletter,* November 1975, p. 3.

Publishers' Weekly 206 (28 October 1974): 47.

Rueckert, William. "Vein of Irony." *New Republic* 172 (5 April 1975): 26–28.

Thomas, Phil. "What is Wrong With Fiction?" *Omaha Sunday World-Herald Magazine,* 2 February 1975, p. 23.

Updike, John, "Wright On Writing." *New Yorker* 51 (14 April 1975): 124–27.

THE CAT'S MEOW. Los Angeles: Black Sparrow Press, 1975 (cloth, paperback).

II. SHORT STORIES

1948 "The Ram in the Thicket." *Harper's Bazaar* 82 (May 1948): 133, 182–94. Reprinted in *National Book Award Reader.* New York: Popular Library, 1966. Also in *Contemporary American Short Stories,* comp. Douglas and Sylvia Angus. Greenwich, Connecticut: Fawcett Publications, Inc., 1967. Also in *Wright Morris: A Reader.* New York: Harper and Row, 1970. Also in *Images of Women in Literature,* comp. Mary Anne Ferguson. Boston: Houghton Mifflin, 1973.
"Where's Justice?" *Cross Section* 1948, ed. Edwin Seaver, pp. 221–30. New York: Simon and Schuster, 1948.

1949 "A Man of Caliber." *Kenyon Review* 11 (Winter 1949): 101–7.
"The Lover." *Harper's Bazaar* 83 (May 1949): 118, 175–80.

1951 "The Sound Tape." *Harper's Bazaar* 85 (May 1951): 125, 175–77.
"The Character of the Lover." *American Mercury* 73 (August 1951): 43–49.

1952 "The Rites of Spring." *New World Writing*, No. 1, pp. 140–45. New York: New American Library, 1952.

1954 "The Safe Place." *Kenyon Review* 16 (Autumn 1954): 587–600. Reprinted in *Gallery of Modern Fiction: Stories from the Kenyon Review*, ed. Robie Macauley. New York: Salem Press, 1966. Also in *Wright Morris: A Reader*. New York: Harper and Row, 1970.

1958 "The Word from Space—A Story." *Atlantic Monthly* 201 (April 1958): 38–42. Reprinted in *Magazine of Science Fiction* 15 (September 1958): 111–18.
"The Cat in the Picture . . . " *Esquire* 49 (May 1958): 90–94.

1959 "Wake Before Bomb." *Esquire* 52 (December 1959): 311–15.

1960 "The Scene." *The Noble Savage*, No. 1, 1960, pp. 60–75.

1966 "Lover, Is That You?" *Esquire* 65 (March 1966): 70, 132–36.

1969 "Since When Do They Charge Admission." *Harper's Magazine* 238 (May 1969): 65–70. Reprinted in *Green Grass, Blue Sky, White House*. Los Angeles: Black Sparrow Press, 1970.
"Drrdla." *Esquire* 72 (August 1969): 87–90. Reprinted in *Green Grass, Blue Sky, White House* (Black Sparrow).
"Green Grass, Blue Sky, White House." *New Yorker* 45 (25 October 1969): 56–62. Reprinted in *Best American Short Stories* 1970, ed. Martha Foley and David Burnett. Boston: Houghton Mifflin, 1970. Also in *Green Grass, Blue Sky, White House* (Black Sparrow).

1970 "How I Met Joseph Mulligan Jr." *Harper's Magazine* 240 (February 1970): 82–85.
"A Fight Between a White Boy and a Black Boy in the Dusk of a Fall Afternoon in Omaha, Nebraska." *New Yorker* 46 (6 June 1970): 109–11. Reprinted in *Here Is Einbaum*. Los Angeles: Black Sparrow Press, 1973.
"Fiona." *Esquire* 74 (July 1970): 106. Reprinted in *Here Is Einbaum* (Black Sparrow).

"Magic." *Southern Review* 6 (Winter 1970): 39–54. Reprinted in *Best American Short Stories* 1971, ed. Martha Foley and David Burnett. Boston: Houghton Mifflin, 1971. Also in *Here Is Einbaum* (Black Sparrow).

1971 "Here is Einbaum." *New Yorker* 47 (26 June 1971): 35–41. Reprinted in *Here Is Einbaum* (Black Sparrow).

1972 "In Another Country." *Atlantic Monthly* 229 (May 1972): 59–62. Reprinted in *Here Is Einbaum* (Black Sparrow).

1973 "Trick or Treat." *Quarterly Review of Literature* 18 (1973): 368–78.
"Real Losses, Imaginary Gains." *New Yorker* 49 (26 November 1973): 46–47.

III. ARTICLES AND REVIEWS BY WRIGHT MORRIS

1951 "An Author's Pleasure." McClurg's *Book News,* May 1951, pp. 29–30.
"The New Criticism." *American Scholar* 20 (Summer 1951): 359. A letter to the editor.
"An American In Paris." *New York Times Book Review,* 9 December 1951, p. 28. A review of H. J. Kaplan's *The Spirit and the Bride.*

1952 "The Violent Land—Some Observations on the Faulkner Country." *Magazine of Art* 45 (March 1952): 99–103.
Girson, Rochelle. "Nebraskan Produces Book No. 7." *Lincoln* (Neb.) *Sunday Journal and Star,* 2 March 1952, p. 7D. Remarks of Wright Morris on publication of *The Works of Love.*
"How Come You Settled Down Here?" *Vogue* 119 (15 April 1952): 74, 117–119.

1957 "The Territory Ahead." *The Living Novel: A Symposium,* ed. Granville Hicks, pp. 120–56. New York: Macmillan, 1957. Reprinted New York: Collier Books, 1962 (paperback). Essay reprinted in *Modern American Fiction; Essays in Criticism,* ed. A. Walton Litz, pp. 338–65. New York: Oxford University Press, 1963. This essay appeared later in a different form in Chapters 1, 2, and 14 of *The Territory Ahead.* New York: Harcourt, Brace and Company, 1958.

"What Was Missing in the Fireworks." *New York Times Book Review,* 1 September 1957, p. 3. A review of Sean O'Faolain's *The Vanishing Hero: Studies of Novelists of the Twenties.*

"Norman Rockwell's America." *Atlantic Monthly* 200 (December 1957): 133–36, 138. This essay appeared later in a different form in Chapter 8 of *The Territory Ahead* (Harcourt, Brace and Company).

1958 "The Ability To Function: A Reappraisal of Fitzgerald and Hemingway." *New World Writing,* No. 13, pp. 34–51. New York: New American Library, 1958.

"Our Endless Plains." *Holiday* 24 (July 1958): 68–69, 138–42.

"Henry James's *The American Scene.*" *Texas Quarterly* 1 (Summer–Autumn 1958): 27–42.

"The Cars In My Life." *Holiday* 24 (December 1958): 45–53.

1959 "Lawrence and the Immediate Present." *A D. H. Lawrence Miscellany,* ed. Harry T. Moore, pp. 7–12. Carbondale: Southern Illinois University Press, 1959. Reprinted from *The Territory Ahead* (Harcourt, Brace and Company).

"Mexican Journey." *Holiday* 26 (November 1959): 50–63.

"Nature Since Darwin." *Esquire* 52 (November 1959): 64–70.

1960 "The Open Road." *Esquire* 53 (June 1960): 98–99.

"Comments by Wright Morris" included with Granville Hicks's review of *Ceremony in Lone Tree, Saturday Review* 43 (9 July 1960): 11.

"Made In U. S. A." *American Scholar* 29 (Autumn 1960): 483–94.

1961 "One Law for the Lion." *Partisan Review* 28 (May–June 1961): 541–51. Reprinted in *The Territory Ahead* as a "Postscript." New York: Atheneum, 1963.

"Conversations in a Small Town." *Holiday* 30 (November 1961): 98, 100, 103, 107, 108.

"National Book Award Address, March 12, 1957." *Critique* 4 (Winter 1961–62): 72–75.

1962 "Man on the Moon." *Partisan Review* 29 (Spring 1962): 241–49.

"Letter From Venice: Shooting the Works." *Partisan Review* 29 (Fall 1962): 578–86.

1963 "The Function of Nostalgia: F. Scott Fitzgerald." *F. Scott Fitzgerald: A Collection of Critical Essays,* ed. Arthur Mizener, pp. 25–31. Englewood Cliffs, New Jersey: Prentice-Hall, 1963. Reprinted from *The Territory Ahead* (Harcourt, Brace and Company).

1964 "Afterword" to Richard Henry Dana. *Two Years Before the Mast,* pp. 376–83. New York: New American Library (Signet), 1964 (paperback).

"Foreword" to Mark Twain. *The Tragedy of Pudd'nhead Wilson,* pp. vii–xvii. New York: New American Library, 1964. Toronto: New American Library of Canada, 1964.

"Death of the Reader." *Nation* 198 (13 January 1964): 53–54. This essay appeared later in a different form in *A Bill of Rites, A Bill of Wrongs, A Bill of Goods.* New York: New American Library, 1968.

"Letter to a Young Critic." *Massachusetts Review* 6 (Autumn–Winter 1964–65): 93–100. A letter originally written to David Madden.

1965 "Introduction" to Sherwood Anderson. *Windy McPherson's Son,* pp. vii–xix. Chicago: University of Chicago Press, 1965.

"The Lunatic, The Lover, and The Poet." *Kenyon Review* 27 (Autumn 1965): 727–37.

1966 "The Origin of a Species, 1942–1957." *Massachusetts Review* 7 (Winter 1966): 121–35.

1967 "How Things Are." *Arts and the Public,* ed. James E.
Miller and Paul D. Herring, pp. 33–52 and 230–53
(*passim*). Chicago: University of Chicago Press, 1967.

1969 "*One Day*: November 22, 1963—November 22, 1967."
Afterwords: Novelists on Their Novels, ed. Thomas
McCormack, pp. 10–27. New York: Harper and Row,
1969.

1970 "The Word Between Them." *Writers as Teachers/Teach-*
ers as Writers, ed. Jonathan Baumbach, pp. 192–201.
New York: Holt, Rinehart and Winston, 1970.

1972 "Babe Ruth's Pocket." *Ford Times,* September 1972.
"Notes from a Venetian Journal." *American Scholar* 41
(Autumn 1972): 578–84.

1974 "Telling It Like It Is: A Triumph and Its Consequences."
The Contemporary Literary Scene 1973, ed. Frank N.
Magill. Englewood Cliffs, New Jersey: Salem Press,
1974.

1975 "Natives, Monsters, and Cliches in the Land of Milk and
Honey." *Bookletter* 2 (1 September 1975): 6–7.
"Work of 'Secret Forces' Keys Remarks by Author."
Kearney (Neb.) *Hub,* 17 October 1975, pp. 1, 12.
Luncheon speech at Nebraska Library Association
Convention.

IV. PHOTO-TEXT MATERIAL AND PHOTOGRAPHS

See also these books (Section I): *The Inhabitants, The Home*
Place, God's Country and My People, and *Love Affair—A Ve-*
netian Journal.

1940 "The Inhabitants." *New Directions in Prose and Poetry*
1940, ed. James Laughlin, pp. 145–80. Norfolk, Connecticut: New Directions, 1940.

"White House." *Twice A Year* 5–6 (Double Issue: Fall–Winter 1940 and Spring–Summer 1941): 11. New York: Twice A Year Press.

"The Inhabitants." *Direction* 3 (November 1940): 12–13.

1941 "Landscape With Figures." *New Directions in Prose and Poetry* 1941, ed. James Laughlin, pp. 253–77. Norfolk, Connecticut: New Directions, 1941.

Devree, Howard. "A Reviewer's Notebook: Brief Comment on Some of the Recently Opened Group and One-Man Shows." *New York Times*, 26 October 1941, Section 9, p. 10, col. 2. A comment on an exhibit of Wright Morris photographs with text at the New School for Social Research.

1947 "The Inhabitants." *Photography* (London), July–August 1947, pp. 26–29.

"The Inhabitants." *Spearhead: 10 Years' Experimental Writing in America*, pp. 191–201. New York: New Directions, 1947.

1948 "American Scene." *New York Times Magazine*, 4 July 1948, pp. 14–15.

"Speaking of Pictures: An Author Remembers His Home Place in Nebraska." *Life Magazine* 25 (26 July 1948): 8–10.

1949 "The Home: Echoes from Empty Houses." *The Nation's Heritage*, vol. 1, no. 3 (1949). 24 photographs without pagination. New York: Heritage Magazine, Inc., 1949.

U. S. Camera Annual 1949, ed. Tom Maloney, p. 30. Photograph, with comment by Lewis Mumford. New York: U. S. Camera Corp., 1949.

"Home Town Revisited." *New York Times Magazine*, 24 April 1949, pp. 24–25.

"Guest of Honour—No. 12—Wright Morris (U. S. A.)." *Photography* (London), July 1949, pp. 14–15.

"The World In The Attic." *Photography* (London), September 1949, pp. 17–26.

"Summer Encore." *New York Times Magazine*, 13 November 1949, pp. 26–27.

"Built With More Than Hands." *New York Times Magazine,* 25 December 1949, pp. 12–13.

1950 "Out of Shoes Come New Feet." *New York Times Magazine,* 11 June 1950, pp. 20–21.

1951 "Privacy as a Subject for Photography." *Magazine of Art* 44 (February 1951): 51–55.

1969 Evans, Walker. "Photography" in *Quality, Its Image in the Arts,* ed. Louis Kronenberger. Pp. 180–81: Wright Morris photograph of kitchen chair with Walker Evans comment. New York: Atheneum, 1969.

1974 Doty, Robert M., ed. *Photography in America.* An exhibit at the Whitney Museum of American Art, November 20, 1974 to January 12, 1975. Wright Morris photographs: pp. 140–41: "Winter, Nebraska." P. 141: "My Uncle Harry." New York: Random House, 1974.

1975 *Wright Morris: Structures and Artifacts; Photographs 1933–1954.* Introd. by Norman A. Geske. Catalog of an exhibit at the Sheldon Memorial Art Gallery, University of Nebraska, Lincoln, October 21 to November 16, 1975. Lincoln: University of Nebraska, Sheldon Memorial Art Gallery, 1975. P. 4: Wright Morris, "Statement." Pp. 110–21: Wright Morris interview with Jim Alinder.

V. GENERAL AND CRITICAL WORKS
ON WRIGHT MORRIS

1951 Warfel, Harry R. *American Novelists of Today,* p. 312. New York: American Book Company, 1951.

1957 Booth, Wayne C. "The Two Worlds in the Fiction of Wright Morris." *Sewanee Review* 65 (Summer 1957): 375–99.

Romanova, Elena. "Zametni o sovremennom amerikanskom romane [Notes on the Modern American Novel]." *Inostrannaja Literatura*, No. 12 (1957): 210–16.

1959 Allen, Gay Wilson. "Wright Morris on Whitman: A Review." *Walt Whitman Review* 5 (June 1959): 33–35.

Howe, Irving. "Mass Society and Post-Modern Fiction." *Partisan Review* 26 (Summer 1959): 420–36.

Carpenter, Frederic I. "Wright Morris and *The Territory Ahead.*" *College English* 21 (December 1959): 147–56.

1960 Fiedler, Leslie. *Love and Death in the American Novel*, pp. 323–24, 471–72. New York: Criterion Books, 1960.

Howard, Leon. *Literature and the American Tradition*, p. 306. Garden City: Doubleday and Company, 1960.

Madden, David. "The Hero and the Witness in Wright Morris' *Field of Vision.*" *Prairie Schooner* 34 (Fall 1960): 263–78.

Van Bebber, Gerd. "Wright Morris." *Lexikon der Weltliteratur im 20. Jahrhundert*, Vol. 2, cols. 464–65. Freiburg: Herder, 1960–61. Translation published in *Encyclopedia of World Literature in the 20th Century*, Vol. 2, p. 429. New York: Frederick Ungar, 1967–71.

1961 Flanagan, John T. "The Fiction of Wright Morris." *Studia Germanica Gandensia* 3 (1961): 209–31.

Lory, Alice A. *Wright Morris and the American Mother.* M.A. thesis, Montana State University, 1961.

Hassan, Ihab. *Radical Innocence: Studies in the Contemporary American Novel*, pp. 6, 78, 101. Princeton, New Jersey: Princeton University Press, 1961. Reprinted New York: Harper and Row, 1966.

Oliphant, Robert. "Public Voices and Wise Guys." *Virginia Quarterly Review* 37 (Autumn 1961): 522–37.

Baumbach, Jonathan. "Wake Before Bomb: Ceremony in Lone Tree." *Critique* 4 (Winter 1961–62): 56–71.

Madden, David. "The Great Plains in the Novels of Wright Morris." *Critique* 4 (Winter 1961–62): 5–23.

Trachtenberg, Alan. "The Craft of Vision." *Critique* 4 (Winter 1961–62): 41–55.

Waterman, Arthur E. "The Novels of Wright Morris: An Escape from Nostalgia." *Critique* 4 (Winter 1961–62): 24–40.

1962 Hunt, John W., Jr. "The Journey Back: The Early Novels of Wright Morris." *Critique* 5 (Spring–Summer 1962): 41–60.

Booth, Wayne C. "The Shaping of Prophecy: Craft and Idea in the Novels of Wright Morris." *American Scholar* 31 (Autumn 1962): 608–26.

Leer, Norman. "Three American Novels and Contemporary Society: A Search for Commitment." *Wisconsin Studies in Contemporary Literature* 3 (Fall 1962): 67–86.

1963 Eisinger, Chester E. "Wright Morris: The Artist in Search for America," in his *Fiction of the Forties*, pp. 328–41. Chicago: University of Chicago Press, 1963.

Allen, Walter. *The Modern Novel in Britain and the United States*, pp. 315–17. New York: Dutton, 1964. Published in England as *Tradition and Dream; the English and American Novel from the Twenties to Our Time*. London: Phoenix House, 1964.

1964 Klein, Marcus. "Wright Morris: The American Territory," in his *After Alienation; American Novels in Mid-Century*, pp. 196–246. Cleveland: World Publishers, 1964.

Madden, David. *Wright Morris*. New York: Twayne Publishers, 1964.

Nyren, Dorothy, comp. *A Library of Literary Criticism: Modern American Literature*, pp. 354–56, 572–74. 3rd ed. New York: Frederick Ungar, 1964. Excerpts from reviews and articles.

1965 Dommergues, Pierre. *Les Ecrivains Américains d'Aujourd'hui*, pp. 106–7, 120. Paris: Presses Universitaires de France, 1965. (Series "Que Sais-Je?")

Shetty, Nalini V. *The Fiction of Wright Morris*. Ph.D. dissertation, University of Pittsburgh, 1965. (Abstract in *Dissertation Abstracts* 27 [1967]: 3471.)

Tucker, Martin. "The Landscape of Wright Morris." *Lock Haven Review* 7 (1965): 43–51.

Waldmeir, Joseph J. " 'Accommodation' in the New Novel." *University College Quarterly* 11 (November 1965): 26–32.

1966 Nelson, Carolyn Williamson. *The Spiritual Quest in the Works of Wright Morris*. Ph.D. dissertation, University of Chicago, 1966.

1967 Hitchings, Sharlene Allyn. *Wright Morris: The Early Nebraska Novels*. M.A. thesis, San Diego State College, 1967.

Shetty, Nalini V. "Of Human Bondage: Captivity in Time and Hero in the Fiction of Wright Morris," pp. 191–207 of *Indian Response to American Literature*, ed. C. D. Narasimhaiah. New Delhi: The United States Educational Foundation in India, 1967.

Miller, James E., Jr. "The Nebraska Encounter: Willa Cather and Wright Morris," *Prairie Schooner* 41 (Summer 1967): 165–67.

Garrett, George. "Morris the Magician: A Look at *In Orbit*." *Hollins Critic* 4 (June 1967): 1–12. Reprinted in *The Sounder Few; Essays from the Hollins Critic*, ed. R. H. W. Dillard, George Garrett, and John R. Moore, pp. 263–80. Athens: University of Georgia Press, 1971.

Kuehl, John, ed. *Write and Rewrite: A Study of the Creative Process*,pp. xii and 308(draft and final version of work by Wright Morris). New York: Meredith Press, 1967.

Hicks, Granville. "Five for Year's End." *Saturday Review* 50 (30 December 1967): 19–20.

1968 Morgan, Steve. *The Will-o-the-Wisp of the Plains in Wright Morris' Works*. M.A. thesis, Municipal University of Omaha, 1968.

Howard, Leon. *Wright Morris*. Minneapolis: University of Minnesota Press, 1968. (University of Minnesota Pamphlets on American Writers, no. 69.)

Guettinger, Roger J. "The Problem with Jigsaw Puzzles:
Form in the Fiction of Wright Morris." *Texas Quarterly* 11 (Spring 1968): 209–20.

Madden, David. "The Fallacy of the Subject-Dominated
Novel." *English Record* 18 (April 1968): 11–19.

Waterman, Arthur E. "Wright Morris's *One Day*: The
Novel of Revelation." *Furman Studies* n.s. 15 (May
1968): 29–36.

Madden, David. "Wright Morris' *In Orbit*: An Unbroken
Series of Poetic Gestures." *Critique* 10 (Fall 1968):
102–19. Reprinted in David Madden. *The Poetic Image
in Six Genres*. Carbondale: Southern Illinois University Press, 1969.

1969 Infanger, Harold. *The Crippling Thralldom of Nostalgia
in Two Nebraska Novels by Wright Morris*. M.S.
thesis, Chadron State College (Nebraska), 1969. Examines *The Home Place* and *The World in the Attic*.

Shetty, Nalini V. "Wright Morris and the Territory
Ahead," pp. 71–83 in *Indian Essays in American Literature: Papers in Honour of Robert E. Spiller*, ed.
Sujit Mukherjee and D.V.K. Raghavacharyulu. Bom-
bay: Popular Prakashan, 1969.

1970 Cohn, Jack Rice. *Wright Morris: The Design of the Mid-
western Fiction*. Ph.D. dissertation, University of
California at Berkeley, 1970. (Abstract in *Dissertation
Abstracts International* 32 [1970]: 960A.)

Crump, Gail Bruce. *Wright Morris and the Immediate
Present*. Ph.D. dissertation, University of Arkansas,
1970. (Abstract in *Dissertation Abstracts International* 31 [1970]: 1267A.)

Hicks, Granville. "Wright Morris," pp. 7–47 of his *Literary Horizons: A Quarter Century of American Fiction*. New York: New York University Press, 1970.
Reprints of his reviews of ten of Wright Morris's
works (noted individually under their original appearances).

Hicks, Granville. "Introduction" to *Wright Morris: A
Reader*, pp. ix–xxxiii. New York: Harper and Row,
1970.

Katona, Anna. *Picaresque Satires in Modern American Fiction*, pp. 114–16. Budapest, Hungary: Akadémiac Kiadó (Publishing House of the Hungarian Academy of Sciences), 1970.

Waldeland, Lynne Maret. *Wright Morris: His Theory and Practice of the Craft of Fiction.* Ph. D. dissertation, Purdue University, 1970. (Abstract in *Dissertation Abstracts International* 31 [1970]: 1819A.)

Aldridge, John W. "*Wright Morris: A Reader.*" (not a review) *New York Times Book Review*, 11 January 1970, pp. 4, 33. Reprinted as "Wright Morris's Reputation," in his *The Devil in the Fire: Retrospective Essays on American Literature and Culture*, 1951–1971, pp. 257–60. New York: Harper's Magazine Press, 1972.

1971 DeMott, Benjamin. "Beyond the Conflict of Generations." *Saturday Review* 54 (21 August 1971): 19–22.

1972 Klein, Marcus. "Wright Morris." *Contemporary Novelists*, pp. 902–4. New York: Saint Martin's Press, 1972.

Richey, Clarence W. " 'The Riverrun': A Note Upon a Joycean Quotation in Wright Morris's *In Orbit.*" *Notes on Contemporary Literature* 2 (January 1972): 14–15.

1973 *Contemporary Literary Criticism*, ed. Carolyn Riley *et al.*, Vol. 1, pp. 230–33; Vol. 3, pp. 342–44. Detroit: Gale Research Company, 1973, 1975. Excerpts from reviews and critical works.

Dymond, Richard Bruce. *The Impoverished Self: A Study of Selected Fiction of Wright Morris.* Ph.D. dissertation, University of Rochester, 1973. (Abstract in *Dissertation Abstracts International* 34 [1973]: 2619A.)

Rooke, Constance. *Character in the Early Fiction of Wright Morris.* Ph.D. dissertation, University of North Carolina at Chapel Hill, 1973. (Abstract in *Dissertation Abstracts International* 34 [1974]: 5990A.)

Waldeland, Lynne Maret. "*The Deep Sleep*: The Fifties in the Novels of Wright Morris," pp. 25–43 in *Silhouettes on the Shade: Images from the 50s Reexamined.* Muncie, Indiana: Ball State University, [1973?].

1974 Madden, David. "Wright Morris." *Cyclopedia of World Authors*, ed. Frank N. Magill, rev. ed., pp. 1274–75. Englewood Cliffs, New Jersey: Salem Press, 1974.

Wilson, James C. *Wright Morris and the Search for the Still Point of the Turning World.* M.A. thesis, University of Nebraska, 1974.

Madden, David. "Morris' *Cannibals, Cain's Serenade*: The Dynamics of Style and Technique." *Journal of Popular Culture* 8 (Summer 1974): 59–70.

1975 Wilson, James C. "Wright Morris and the Search for the 'Still Point'." *Prairie Schooner* 49 (Summer 1975): 154–63.

Sheldon, Robert. "The Art of Wright Morris." *Nebraska Alumnus*, November–December 1975, pp. 6–9.

Ferguson, Linda W. "A Morris Marathon." *Pacific Sun Literary Quarterly*, 28 November 1975, pp. 17, 24.

VI. BIOGRAPHICAL AND BIBLIOGRAPHICAL MATERIAL

1940 *Direction* 3 (November 1940): 1. A biographical note.

1942 "Wright Morris Writes 'My Uncle Dudley'." *Lincoln* (Neb.) *Sunday Journal and Star*, 3 May 1942, p. 5D.

Busch, Arthur J. "Fellowships for Photography." *Popular Photography* 2 (October 1942): 22–23, 82.

1949 "Two-Gun Man." *New York Times Book Review*, 28 August 1949, p. 8.

1951 "Main Line Author of the Month." *Main Line*, June 1951, pp. 24, 41–42.

Hutchins, John K. "On an Author." *New York Herald Tribune Book Review*, 3 June 1951, p. 2.

Breit, Harvey. "Talk with Wright Morris." *New York Times Book Review*, 10 June 1951, p. 19.

1955 Kunitz, Stanley J., ed. "Wright Morris," in *Twentieth Century Authors*, First Supplement, pp. 691–92. New York: H. W. Wilson, 1955.

1957 "Publishing Group Honors 3 Writers." *New York Times,* 13 March 1957, p. 28, col. 6. A notice of Wright Morris's winning the National Book Award for 1957 for *The Field of Vision.*

1958 Davis, Robert Gorham. "Readers and Writers Face to Face." *New York Times Book Review,* 9 November 1958, pp. 4, 40–41. Wright Morris participated in a symposium, "The Role of the Writer in America," held at Columbia University by Esquire Magazine and the Writers' Club of the School of General Studies, Columbia University.

1959 Bleufarb, Sam. "Point of View: An Interview with Wright Morris, July 1958." *Accent* 19 (Winter 1959): 34–46.

1960 Knox, Sanka. "2 Art Groups Give $40,000 in Awards." *New York Times,* 26 May 1960, p. 38, col. 6. A notice of a National Institute of Arts and Letters grant to Wright Morris.

1961 Linden, Stanton J. and Madden, David. "A Wright Morris Bibliography." *Critique* 4 (Winter 1961–62): 77–87.

1965 Kovacsi, Gabor. "An Interview with Wright Morris." *Plum Creek Review* (Oberlin College, Ohio), Spring 1965, pp. 36–40.
Young, David P. "Wright Morris in Oberlin." *Plum Creek Review* (Oberlin College, Ohio), Spring 1965, pp. 17–18.

1966 "John Simon Guggenheim Memorial Foundation Fellows in Photography, 1937–1965." *Camera* 45 (April 1966): 6, 16–17.

1967 Dommergues, Pierre. *Les U. S. A. à la Recherche de Leur Identité: Rencontres avec 40 Ecrivains Américains,* pp. 37–38, 57–58, 453. Paris: Bernard Grasset, 1967.

1973 Pfeil, Fred. "Querencias, and a Lot Else: An Interview with Wright Morris." *Place* 3 (June 1973): 53–63.

1974 Haydn, Hiram. *Words and Faces,* pp. 228–33. New York: Harcourt, Brace, Jovanovich, 1974.

1975 "Interview: Wright Morris." *Great Lakes Review* 1 (Winter 1975): 1–29.

Haggie, Helen. "Wright Morris Plans Semester at University." *Lincoln,* (Neb.) *Sunday Journal and Star, Focus Magazine of Nebraska,* 4 May 1975, pp. 1F, 8H.

Boyce, Robert L. "Wright Morris." *Nebraska Library Association Quarterly* 6 (Fall 1975): 23–24.

Morris, Wright. "The Mari Sandoz Acceptance Speech." *Nebraska Library Association Quarterly* 6 (Winter 1975): 4–5. Speech on acceptance of the Association's Mari Sandoz Award, October 16, 1975.

"Caption Aids Picture's Value." *Lincoln* (Neb.) *Journal,* 22 October 1975, p. 57.

"Bunnell Lauds Morris Photos." *Lincoln* (Neb.) *Journal,* 8 November 1975, p. 3.

Wade, Gerald. "For A Time, Wright Morris Comes Home." *Omaha Sunday World-Herald Magazine of the Midlands,* 7 December 1975, pp. 16, 18, 20.

Index